GUINNESS
TIMES

GUINNESS TIMES

MY DAYS IN THE WORLD'S MOST FAMOUS BREWERY

AL BYRNE

TOWN
HOUSE
DUBLIN

First published in 1999
by
Town House and Country House
Trinity House, Charleston Rd
Ranelagh, Dublin 6

ISBN: 1-86059-105-1

Copyright © Al Byrne 1999

A CIP catalogue record for this book is available from the British Library.

Cover design by Jason Ellams
Typeset by Typeform Repro Ltd, Dublin
Printed in Italy

To my wife Frances, who, in spite of having listened to me talking about Guinness for over forty years, provided the necessary encouragement, understanding, saintly patience and TLC to enable me to write this book

Acknowledgements

I drew material for this book from three main sources. One was documentary (books – the main ones are listed at the back of this book – and photographs); the second was oral and aural; the third was my faulty, wayward and mischievous memory

Special thanks to the Guinness archivist, Teresa O'Donnell, and to the following Guinness personnel, current or retired: Pat Barry, Harry Hannon, Michael Lawlor, Dr Brendan McCarthy, Don Mooney, David Orr, Billy Porter, Nancy Richards (Guinness Publishing London), Carol Scott, Richard Westrup, Anne Whelan; and to the Guinness Ireland Group who generously placed at my disposal files, documents, books, photographs and so on.

Thanks also to my daughter, Hilary Byrne, for keeping the floppy discs safe and for many imaginative suggestions; to my son, Ian Byrne, for several sensible suggestions for changes to the typescript; to Ciaran Nicholson, Trinity College Library; the Press Office of the Central Bank of Ireland; and to the governor of the Bank of Ireland.

To all those people who have generously given me of their time, knowledge, experience and guidance I offer my most sincere thanks. And to all those who should be mentioned here and are inexcusably not, I offer my sincere apologies. It's that inefficient memory of mine!

Contents

Foreword

Many books have been written about Guinness. Individually and collectively these contain an immense amount of very interesting information, facts, comment and opinion about Guinness – the product, the family, the Company and some of its personnel, the Brewery itself. So why another book about Guinness?

Because I believe that one of the aspects of the whole Guinness story has never been adequately written about. There is little or no record of what it was like to work full-time at St James's Gate. There has been virtually no telling of the place itself and its ethos, the kind of people who worked there at all levels in the hierarchical personnel structure, the type of work they did, the myriad activities they engaged in which had an umbilical connection with their main jobs.

Because working at St James's Gate was not so much a job as a whole way of life. And, for the first time as experienced by an insider, I want to tell what this was like and its place in the whole extraordinary story of a man called Guinness and the world-famous beer he invented. By any standards, it is an extraordinary story. It stretches back 240 years to the time the beer was first made in Ireland to the present day when it is brewed in fifty-one countries and consumed world-wide at the rate of 10 million glasses every day.

At the same time it is important to tell something of the environment in which the Guinness company found itself, because without having some sense of what Dublin and Ireland were like in the period under review, this version of the story of Guinness would be quite incomplete.

Why me to write the story? A few reasons. First of all I entered St James's Gate as a boy messenger in 1938. I retired from it at senior management level in 1978. Coming from shop floor to management meant that I was involved at virtually all levels of operations – including working directly with members of the Guinness family. In addition to working within the walls I spent many years working directly for the Company outside the gates in areas such as sales, promotions, broadcasting and PR. I know of nobody else who has had that particular quantity, quality and variety of experience.

Secondly, my time with Guinness was a critical time for the Company. For more than a century, before 1938, very little change of any great import took place – except the major change from a strictly family concern to a public company in 1886. After 1978 not only was change going on but it was going on at an ever-accelerating rate, culminating in the Company's being subsumed into Diageo in 1997.

But the forty-year period between 1938 and 1978 (my time with the Company) was very interesting indeed. It had enough of the old to experience and enjoy. It had enough of the bridge between old and new to make it fascinating and exciting. And it had enough of the new to make it challenging and stimulating – albeit tinged with sadness for *les temps perdus*. And it was my good fortune to be there at just the right time. Not only did I observe it all happening but I was directly involved in the design and implementation of some of the changes.

Thirdly, as far as I can ascertain, I was the subject of a number of 'firsts' – most of which were entirely outside my control. I was the first person to be appointed to the No. I Staff who had the following combination of characteristics: (a) I was a Roman Catholic, (b) I was classified in the Company's books as a 'labourer', (c) I was a graduate of Trinity College Dublin and (d) I had a father working in Guinness who was also a Roman Catholic and classified as a 'labourer'. It was not any one of these things alone but the combination which, apparently, constituted a 'first'. It seems that I have an interesting – perhaps even unique – point of view on Guinness.

Lastly, I am a working journalist and so I should be able to write about it.

The format I've chosen is that of the odyssey. I invite the reader to come with me on a journey down forty years in and around St James's Gate. This brewery was once the biggest in the world. During my Guinness days it was (and remains to this day) one of the world's biggest breweries, the biggest in Europe, and the biggest exporting brewery in the world. It is also the most famous brewery in the world.

If you come with me on this trip, I'll have pleasure in taking you down countless bye-ways and boreens to show you the myriad goings-on and the fascinating people who worked there in that unique place called St James's Gate. I hope you will find it interesting.

Entering St James's Gate

It was 8.45am on 21 March 1938 when I entered the Back Gate of the Guinness Brewery at St James's Gate in Dublin. I was fourteen years old, and I was terrified.

I had been to Mass (it was the feast of St Benedict), had a good breakfast and then walked along the canal which more or less linked our home at Rialto to St James's Gate. I was spick and span in my knee-length pants, open-necked shirt, jacket and boots. Because my father had served with the Irish Guards before and during World War I, all four boys in our family had to turn out more or less on parade each morning before going to school or work and pass the test of 'Fit to go out?' (It took me a long time to understand why my only sister Mary did not have to go on parade.) Anyway, on this particular morning, I passed with flying colours.

But there was another reason why I had to look my best going into the Brewery on that morning. It was because my father, two of his brothers, one of my own brothers and countless cousins worked there, so I had a family reputation to keep up and no nonsense about it. There would be no excuse for anything less than a good performance in every way.

I didn't know it at the time, but I was being introduced to the positively fierce sense of loyalty that existed among people who worked in the Company. In many cases, having a job with Guinness was a father-to-son practice. In this, the employees were merely following the family's own practice of two centuries' standing. It had worked extremely well for them. Employees could do worse than follow suit, it seemed.

Boys in the Brewery

Every year Guinness recruited boys of fourteen to work in the Brewery. Because of its location, almost all those who applied came from Dublin and most of them were pupils at one or other of the Christian Brothers schools in the city. Some boys in these schools, and most boys in other Dublin schools, remained at school until they were sixteen (when they did their Intermediate Certificate exam) or until they were eighteen (when they sat their Leaving Certificate exam). These were the boys whose families could afford to keep them at school until they either went to university or got a job in the civil service or in banks or insurance companies.

My family, which consisted of my parents plus five children, could not afford to keep me or my eldest brother Ray or my younger brother Ernest at school beyond the age of fourteen. We had to go out and find a job. Ray got a job as a laboratory assistant in the research laboratory in Guinness. When my turn came I got a job as a boy messenger there also.

Since competition was very keen, we were lucky to have made it. The routine was that the Company made it known that they were about to hold what they called an 'Open Competitive Examination' to recruit laboratory attendants, boy messengers and boy labourers. You wrote in and applied. You were then instructed to come and sit the examination – which was in the usual school subjects plus General Information. Then you waited for the results. If successful (and that meant you were one of about ten boys out of a total of a hundred or so applicants), you were called for an interview.

You were asked many questions and your answers were written down on a form. Then you were asked what turned out to be probably the crucial question: 'Does your father work here?' If you said no, then a large stamp was thumped on your form which read 'Son of Outsider'. It wasn't exactly a mark of 'Untouchable' but it didn't help your prospects. On the other hand, the stamp put on forms like mine said 'Son of Employee'. That was comforting for me. And, in retrospect, comforting for the Company, because they reasoned that, if the father of a job-seeking boy had a good record in the Company, then the chances were that his son would be suitable. Call it nepotism, but it worked!

If you passed this interview test you had one more mountain to climb. This was the medical exam. You went to the Guinness Dispensary and were examined by a Company doctor. The worst moment for the poor little fourteen-year-olds was the command 'Drop your pants... cough... umm... fine... pull up your pants.' (I suppose this was to confirm your gender, but perhaps it was to check you out for hernia.)

Back then to the interviewer to be told the worst or the best. I was in! I waltzed home and gave the good news to my mother. Heaven was thanked. A rosary was said. My wages would be a pound a week. But the Company stopped one-and-a-penny a week for insurance. That meant that my weekly take-home was eighteen shillings and elevenpence. I would, my mother said, be allowed to keep the elevenpence, but I had to give her the eighteen shillings. She was delighted. Quite a little bit more in the weekly coffers to feed and clothe the family. As for me – I was going to be as rich as Croesus! And I was to start earning this fortune by coming to the back gate at 8.45am on 21 March. So that's how and why I joined the queue that morning.

My first day at work

The queue moved rapidly and as each person reached the guichet he shouted a number and was given a little brass disc with that number on it. When my turn came I just gawked helplessly at the man behind the glass. 'What's your number, son?' He was nice. I said I had no number. 'You'd better come in and we'll deal with you later.' That 'deal with' frightened me. But I need not have worried. I went into his office and was quite dazzled at the walls covered in brass numbers. Everyone was shouting out numbers. The brass discs were very noisy. There was laughter and crack. I was enjoying myself.

Eventually the queue was gone. Except for a very few left over, the discs were gone too. The man filled in a form about who I was. Then he gave me a disc with a warning not to lose it or there would be a dreadful row. I was No. 50.

HEALTH AND WELFARE AT GUINNESS

In 1870, decades before organised medical care was introduced by industry or government, the Guinness Dispensary was set up at St James's Gate to care, free of charge, for the health of all employees and their dependent families. Medical staff consisted of a doctor, an assistant doctor who was also a pharmaceutical chemist, a part-time secretary, a Lady Visitor for the supervision of the widows, and a midwife. A daily dispensary was held, free medicines were dispensed, and visits by a doctor were paid to the homes of employees and their dependants who were too ill to attend the dispensary.

In the year 1880, attendances at the Dispensary amounted to 19,000 and home visits were 2206. In all, the infant Medical Department was looking after 15,000 people. By the early 1940s, the Medical Department had grown. It moved into bigger and better premises at St James's Gate. Staff had increased to include three doctors, two dentists, two pharmaceutical chemists, a physio-therapist, a welfare superintendent, four clerks, two waiting-room attendants and so on. Modern equipment was installed. Yearly attendance had reached 60,000 and annual prescriptions issued rose to 100,000.

The man whose name will always live in the history of the Medical Department came to it in 1884. His name was Dr John Lumsden, and he went on to become the Chief Medical Officer at Guinness. He later became Sir John Lumsden and he left a legacy of splendid work.

The Welfare Department of Guinness was established in 1893. The Welfare Superintendent was a nurse, whose job was to care for the 730 widows of deceased Guinness employees plus 230 orphans. They were visited regularly and given orders for fuel, groceries, flannel and milk. They were offered loans. The children were given advice about and help with getting jobs. Young widows were offered jobs as office cleaners at St James's Gate at a weekly rate of twenty-eight shillings. Weekly pensions of sixteen shillings were paid to widows of employees plus a weekly allowance of three shillings and sixpence a week for each child up to the age of fifteen.

This Welfare Superintendent lived on the premises at St James's Gate and was available at all hours of the day and night. Even as long ago as the turn of the century she was involved in trying to sort out family rows — in essence, the beginning, almost a hundred years ago, of family or marriage counselling.

Then he made a phone call, and a few minutes later I was collected by a uniformed boy messenger and taken across the Brewery yard to where my base camp was.

It was in No. 1 Thomas Street — the very house that was on the site of the brewery bought by the first Arthur Guinness in 1759. He had made it into his town house. It was now turned into an office block, but, typical of Guinness, they kept the beautiful wooden floors, doors, stairways and windows. It was all highly polished and lovely.

Then I met my boss. He was a man of fifty or so and he was dressed in uniform — black boots, dark serge trousers with red piping down the sides, dark serge buttoned-up jacket and a cap. And he had a strange array of little coloured flags above his breast pocket. I found out later that he had been in the war, a sergeant in the Royal Dublin Fusiliers, and had been wounded in Gallipoli. The little flags signified the medals he had won.

His first words to me were few: 'Are you Byrne?' I said I was. That was about it. I was handed over with the introduction, 'This is Butcher. He'll train you for a week and after that you'll be on your own.' And this little incident was my first lesson in the hierarchical structure at St James's Gate. In fairness, with about five thousand people working there, some form of structure was absolutely essential. From that first hour or so in St James's Gate, it became obvious to me that the place was run on army lines. And I had come in at rock bottom — a rookie!

Family Life

Family life and my career at Guinness are inextricably intertwined, so let me pause for a moment to tell you a little about my family and what became of us all.

The Byrnes

Of the seven members of my immediate family four of us worked in Guinness – my father, my brother Ray, my sister Mary and myself. In addition, two of my uncles and very many of my cousins worked there. This sort of family connection with the Company was very common. Guinness had always been a family business, was a family business during my innings of forty years, and continued to be so until 1986 when Benjamin, the last family member to be chairman, handed over to an outsider, Ernest Saunders.

My maternal grandparents (whose name was Carroll) died before I was born. They had at least six children. I say 'at least' because, in those days (1880–1910), the rate of infant mortality in Ireland was fairly high. They lived in a tiny cottage near the Dargle River in Bray, County Wicklow. My mother, Anne Carroll, was the youngest of the family.

From distaff to spear-side. We are now in the Earl of Meath's estate at Kilruddery, Bray, in County Wicklow. We are in the era of horse-drawn vehicles and one of the coachmen was Alexander Byrne – my grandfather. In 1876 he married a local girl, Mary Anne Doyle. They lived in a beautiful lodge, which went with the job, on the estate. The name of the lodge was Giltspur. It was called after the two mountains nearby – Big and Little Sugarloaf. When the sun shines on them they look like two golden spurs — or giltspurs. Hence Giltspur. The house I live in today is called Gilspur after my granny's lodge.

My grandparents produced ten children — nine males and one female. Of those nine male children, eight joined the British Army and served in the 1914–18 war. They were big, handsome chaps and when they came home on furlough and in uniform and strolled around Bray town the local girls became quite distracted with excitement. One of them was my mother. And so it came to pass that, on 6 July 1917, Corporal Edward Byrne of the Irish Guards (subsequently the 19th Hussars) married Anne Carroll.

What were they like? And what kind of children were the six that they produced? In our home, my mother had the dominant gene. In a quiet, unsung way she was a remarkable woman. She was tough, practical, efficient, caring, proud. She instilled into all of us a belligerent independence: 'You can go hungry but you must never owe anybody anything,' she would tell us. And she couldn't quite hide from us a definite streak of romanticism and 'if only'. She loved us all, and she tilled the land of our predispositions by sowing the seeds of discontent. She encouraged us to get up and go, and she did it by gentling us into the frame of mind of not being satisfied with what we had. In her own way she called that 'creative drive'. And, call it what you will, this much can be said of it: it distinguished the self-helpers from the supine.

And my father? He was born on 9 November 1892.

On that day, 26 years later, the defeated kaiser abdicated and my father would claim that the eight Byrne soldiers were partially responsible for his defeat! He went through the hell of the trenches. I have his war medals and some splendid pictures of him in uniform. One of my great regrets is that I didn't talk more to him. We talked a lot — but not enough. And it's too late now.

He loved my mother. They were very happily married. And he loved us. He was a simple but sensitive man. He had developed his own philosophy of life which meant, in essence, that having survived the war he was now safely on borrowed time and the thing to do was enjoy it. In or around 1919, like many another demobbed Irish 'tommy', he got a job in Guinness in Dublin and there he stayed all his working life until he died of oesophageal cancer in July 1953. My mother never recovered from his death.

Of the six Byrne children, the first-born died within a few days of birth. Of the one female and four males who survived, the most heroic act of survival was that of our only sister, Mary. By that I mean that any girl who grew up with four Byrne boys, gave as good as she got, and lived to tell the tale, is nothing short of heroic.

We were a typical Dublin working-class family. We were totally orthodox Roman Catholics with a highly religious mother. My father was the sole earner and, even with overtime and some Sunday work, income was extremely tight. We lived in a rented Dublin Artisans' Dwelling Company (DADC) house in Rialto Street —

which connects South Circular Road with the Grand Canal. The DADC was a company founded in the late 1870s and run by Protestant business men and it paid a modest 4% dividends to its shareholders. Among the largest investors was the Guinness family. In 1883, Edward Cecil Guinness requested the DADC to build a large, three-storey block of tenements for Guinness workers at Rialto and in 1889 they also built a small housing estate around this block. At the same time the block and estate became the property of the DADC and our rented house was on that little estate. One result of the Guinness background was that many Guinness employees lived in Rialto Street. In fact, the story is that, at one time, there was a large bell in the tenement block which was rung early every morning to wake up the Guinness workers. This bell is now in the Guinness Museum.

Family life and family finances

We lived like thousands of other families at that time in Dublin. You could buy a small rabbit for fourpence. Or you could buy a large one for sixpence. Every Saturday we had rabbit stew for our midday meal and everything but the kitchen sink went into that stew. Carrots, onions, potatoes, parsley, thyme, leftovers – the lot. I mention the cost of the rabbits partly to sharp-focus on the tight family budget and one incident will illustrate what I mean. Normally we bought two sixpenny rabbits, but one time when our sister Mary was in hospital with a kidney infection, my mother's instructions were to get one sixpenny and one fourpenny rabbit. We had one less mouth to feed that week, and twopence saved was twopence saved after all.

It was fourpence to get into the afternoon session of the pictures. You got ten sweets for a penny. A farthing was a quarter of a penny and you got two sweets for a farthing. We teased the girl in our local sweet shop by asking for 'a farthing's worth of mixed sweets'. She eventually got the better of us brats by taking our farthing, putting two sweets on the counter, and saying 'There's the two sweets, mix them yourselves!'

A penny ticket on the bus or tram brought you almost anywhere in Dublin. Ninepence got you a seat in the gods in the Gaiety Theatre. My pal Frank and I went every Saturday night during a season when, thanks to the likes of MacLiammoir and Edwards we saw the works of Ibsen, Shaw, Wilde, Shakespeare, O'Casey, Chekov. When the drama season was over we watched the Dublin Grand Opera Society present *La Traviata, Il Trovatore, Cavaleria Rusticana, Madame Butterfly*. And all of this for ninepence a time – small wonder that some of us got stage-struck!

We played soccer in Rialto Street. Coats went down as goal posts and a sixpenny rubber ball was bliss if we could (collectively) afford it. It didn't matter how many kids turned up – you just divided the lot by two and that was it. Two things could stop a match and clear the street in seconds. One was when the ball broke a window in some house. There was a frozen moment at the awful sound of broken glass and then, suddenly, the street was empty. Not a soul to be seen. For weeks afterwards football was banned in the street.

The other match-stopper was the panic scream 'Look out – it's a rozzer.' That was our word for a policeman, and one would suddenly appear on a bike. Potential international soccer stars would scatter terrorised in all directions and at incredible speed because we genuinely believed that to be caught playing football in the street meant at least six months in jail. It didn't of course, but we weren't to know that.

A few of us had an eye for the girls in the street. Of course you didn't talk about it because anything to do with girls made you a sissy. You were unmanly and somehow or other you were letting the rest of the lads down. In today's terms you had ceased to be macho. So the chisellers playing football on our street could pine away for the love of some thirteen-year-old blonde bombshell from a few doors down but you must not let that be seen and you would certainly never talk about it.

Our scarce financial resources meant that as each of us finished our primary school education we had to leave school and get a job. The first one off the plank was the eldest, Ray, who worked in Guinness as a laboratory attendant. Wages were a pound a week – but slightly reduced because of having to pay insurance. I was next to go into Guinness. That meant a further upping of household income. Next came our brother Ernest – three years younger than me. He tried and failed to get into Guinness

and settled instead for apprenticeship as a cinematograph operator – a title which always sounded too grandiose for someone who simply spun films in a cinema. However, it was a turning point in the household for two reasons. One was that we were literally growing up and we needed more space. The second was the question of secondary education for the two youngest siblings – Mary and Gay.

How my mother managed it we never knew but we moved out of Rialto Street and around the corner on to South Circular Road which gave us more room and even a small back garden. It meant a higher rent, so my mother took in a lodger for a short time.

This major change in our family living meant several things. The increase in total household income secured secondary education for the two tail-enders. The working members of the family had secure jobs and secure wages. The house was much bigger and more comfortable. And there was a sense of 'moving up' socially – something that pleased my mother greatly.

These were the conditions in our home around about the late thirties and early forties. We were comfortable, well-housed, well-fed, and with well-patched but clean clothes. We had no money for luxuries. We did go to the pictures once a week. We played our games. We had our friends. But time marched on and things changed.

Growing up, moving on

At the start of the 1939–40 war Ray joined the Irish army

and served for a couple of years. Then he left and joined the Royal Air Force, where he served until the war was over. All the time he was away Guinness paid half his weekly wages to my mother. He met and married an English girl in the Women's Auxiliary Air Force and, over the next thirty years or so, they lived in London, the United States, Ireland and Canada. He never came back to live at home. Ray's career was in television. They have three daughters, all married and living in Canada. Joyce died in 1996. Ray died in 1998.

Next down the line, after me, came Ernest. He left the cinema job and joined the Royal Air Force. On demob he came home for a very short while and then emigrated to the US. He never came home to live after that. He served with the American army in Korea and, on demob, went into what proved to be a highly successful career in American television. When RTÉ (Radio Telefís Éireann) television opened in December 1961 he was appointed executive producer of the station. Two years later he resigned and returned to the US. He died there of a heart attack in 1983 and left a wife and four children.

Our sister Mary left school at sixteen and studied at a secretarial college. She went into Guinness as a secretary in 1950, and she married David Orr, a No. 1 Staff man. Later, when he went on the road as a Guinness traveller, they moved to live in Ballinasloe and then Sligo before coming back to live in Dublin. They have one son and three daughters. David has now retired and they live partly in Dublin and partly in Inistioge in County Kilkenny.

ILL-HEALTH IN 1940S DUBLIN

In the 1940s dental problems were common, and it was discovered that a great deal of ill-health (for example, rheumatism, digestive disorders and infective disorders) arose from dental defects and sepsis and, since many men, women and children had appalling teeth, treatment of teeth and mouths was very important. Peptic ulcer was another very common disease in the Dublin of the 1940s and also in Guinness. Infectious diseases like diphtheria were widespread and, to make matters worse, it was very difficult to persuade parents to have their children inoculated against it. In the Dublin of the 1930s and early 1940s, the incidence of veneral diseases was on the decline, but the incidence increased again with the war.

But right at the top of the list of most common and most serious diseases came tuberculosis. Two of the major causes were bad housing (including appalling sanitation) and bovine tuberculosis. In 1943, it was reckoned that at least twenty-five per cent of all deaths in Ireland came from tuberculosis, and the Guinness Medical Department set out to reduce the morbidity rate of this scourge by tackling the two fundamental sources of the problem. At the same time they did all they could to treat Company victims of this curse by providing early X-ray diagnosis, education, and beds in sanitoria. Meantime, at national level, Guinness was involved in the setting up of the Irish National Anti-Tuberculosis League.

Gay completed his secondary school education in Synge Street CBS, got his leaving certificate, failed in his attempt to join the No. 1 Staff in Guinness and went into insurance for a few years. After that he opted for a career in broadcasting, both in the UK and Ireland. He married Kathleen Watkins in 1964 and they have two daughters. The family, including Gay himself, have always been glad that he 'wasn't good enough' to get an appointment to the Guinness staff. He has just retired from his major role in Irish broadcasting.

One of the things which may seem odd is that all four brothers found themselves in careers in communications – mostly in television. Somehow or other it seems that we had a pressing need to communicate. We wanted to say things to other people. We joined drama groups, debating societies, choirs. We wrote articles, short stories, scripts, plays, books. All four went, almost as a right, into broadcasting. All four ended up doing a mixture of performance in front of a microphone plus the work behind the scenes. Nobody knows where this desire and propensity to communicate came from but, since four of the five siblings have it, maybe it's in the genes.

How was it that, out of a huge number of families just like ours, the Byrnes seem to have done fairly well? I believe that there are at least two major ingredients which you have to have to achieve your ambitions. One is a great deal of damned hard work and the health and steely determination to stay the course come what may.

The other ingredient is luck. You can exhaust yourself trying to achieve something but if luck runs against you then all is in vain. But you need the luck plus the hard work and, in all truth, the Byrnes did work hard and we were lucky – well most of us were. And that's the way we were brought up. We worked hard to achieve things but undoubtedly one of the great rewards of working hard is not so much the acquisition of material goods as recompense, but the sheer joy of work satisfaction. It's the honourable sense of having done something worth while. And to quote an Americanism 'If you haven't tried it – don't knock it!'

But now, back to my stint in Guinness, and I will begin by explaining how the company was structured, not only because that is interesting in itself, but because it is very relevant to my own story, as we shall see.

The Guinness Hierarchy

The Board

To begin with there was the Supreme Command HQ, otherwise known simply as the Board. There were some five or six directors on this Board, but their names were rarely mentioned, partly because they acted in a collegiate way and partly because their names would have meant nothing to us anyway. They were gods and whatever it was they did they did it in the Board Room. This was a room big enough to run a ballroom-dancing competition in. It was the holy of holies. Board members never seemed to leave their quarters and the only way we knew that they were still alive was when an occasional edict would issue. These took the form of a sheet or more of dark brown paper and the statement on it always began 'The Board has decided…'

Board members were highly educated men of impeccable honour and intentions. They discovered early on that the product they were making and selling was a winner and that the thing to do was simply to maintain the status quo. Don't disturb a winning streak. This attitude of management before, during and after World War II is best illustrated by a remark authoritatively attributed to a managing director of the Company that 'life at the Dublin brewery had been almost offensively easy before 1939'. After all, they could argue, it was an approach that had worked extremely well for over two hundred years, so its case was proven. At any rate there they were – the High Command of St James's Gate. Secure and happy. And they had their own lunch room and, of course, their own lavatory.

Brewers

Next down from the Board of Directors came what was known as 'staff'. Collectively these were the commissioned ranks. And the most senior of these were classified as 'Brewers'. The procedure for appointing Brewers went back a very long way and eventually settled into a habit of almost always appointing British chaps from Oxford or Cambridge. The thinking behind this strange arrangement is difficult to understand but it certainly had a lot to do with who you knew besides what you knew. An appointment as a Brewer didn't necessarily depend on a knowledge of brewing!

For the most part (and there were some marvellous exceptions) these Brewers were harmless enough. They were decent, well-educated chaps who were perceived as swanning around in shabby tweed jackets, flannel bags and scuffed shoes as if trying to find a problem for some solution they had made up in a laboratory. They were once described by a very wholesome director as 'mostly first-class passengers'. In fairness to them, their real problem was that they were encouraged to think and act as if they were frightfully important. Throughout the Company's existence, most directors had joined the Board via the Brewers' list; in other words they had come into the Company as Brewers, as that was the best route to the Board.

It was top management who designed and executed the system whereby every department, brewing or otherwise, had a Brewer at its top. The fact that most of the time the Brewer in charge of any department other than brewing didn't have the faintest idea of the intricacies of the department's work didn't seem to have captured the attention of the Board.

Take as an example the Forwarding Department. This department was responsible for the transportation of all outgoing supplies of stout and the return of all empties to St James's Gate. The work required professional knowledge of transport matters and, to help the Guinness staff, the Company hired people from outside to come in and do the job of designing and managing this activity. But at the head of this department was a brewer, with the title 'Brewer-in-charge, Forwarding Department'. He knew virtually nothing about transport. And the imported professionals had to cope with this nonsense – certainly a case of faulty management practices in a company where criticism was not allowed.

In the 1890s the starting salary of a Brewer was £100 *per annum* – but rising by £100 *per annum* until they reached £1000 *per annum* within ten years. Compare that with the average wage for a labourer of about £75 a year, while a tradesman got about £150 a year. But maintenance of high standards and constant close monitoring of the product was most important and, rightly, Brewers were very high up in the pecking order. They were senior and mostly dull, and they too had their own 'Brewers' Luncheon Room'.

No. 1 Staff

Next down in seniority came the 'No. 1 Staff'. Again, these were senior commissioned officers who had jobs as accountants, administrators, brewing staff, trade representatives, chemists, engineers, general management. In effect, collectively, they ran the Brewery. They had their own lavatories, clearly marked as such. They also had a very large Guinness house in James's Street, which was used mostly by their members on shift work (brewing is a process which never stops), complete with drawing room, bedrooms, radio, showers and squash court.

Like the Brewers, almost all members of this No. 1 Staff came from outside the Company and entry at eighteen or nineteen years of age was by way of an open competitive exam, together with an interview and references. All quite normal and effective. It kept out the undesirables, allowed in the desirables and resulted in taking in (mostly) high-class individuals who (mostly) went on to prove that the selection process worked very well.

Some of those who came in went on later to distinguish themselves in the world outside Guinness. Some who stayed went on to be departmental managers and, in the case of a few, directors of the Company. Some of them who went straight from school into line management learned very quickly (like many a subaltern) how to handle men. It was a lesson to be grateful for and to keep in mind.

A small but symbolic point. As with Brewers, members of the No. 1 Staff had the great plus of being able to sign a

MAKING GUINNESS

The water used in producing Guinness does not come from the River Liffey or from a canal. It comes from St James's Well in County Kildare. Because of its purity and softness, and its individual flavour, this water is ideally suitable for the making of Guinness.

Malt starts its life as barley. Guinness is constantly researching the best types of barley for its purposes. Apart from the cost of barley research the Guinness Company pays about £15m a year to Irish farmers for the entire barley requirements of St James's Gate – amounting to some 90,000 tonnes.

To 'malt' a barley, you first steep the barley grains in water, and they will gradually begin to swell. Then they start to sprout little shoots. That's a sign that changes are taking place within the barley grains and the process of conversion of starch into sugar has started. At that point the barley is dried by controlled heat. The finished dried product is malt.

This malt is then ground up, a little roasted malt is added to give it a dark colour, and it is mixed with hot water to make a porridge-like mess. When this is thoroughly mashed you drain off the liquid from it and you have a substance called 'wort', a sugary liquid that is ready for the next stage of brewing.

Hops is a climbing, perennial plant whose flowers are gathered in the hop fields of England, North America, Germany and Australia, and taken to breweries all over the world – including St James's Gate. There in the Brewery the hops are boiled with the wort and the resultant liquid is drained off. The hops have three main functions. One is to give a bitter flavour to the beer. The second is to give it an attractive aroma. And the third is that hops act as a natural preservative.

Now we have hopped wort all ready to be turned into beer. What it needs to achieve this conversion is yeast. Yeast cells require food to survive and multiply and, in brewing, they get their food from the sugar in hopped wort.

Yeast can be temperamental, and it has to be handled with care. It has strong family affiliations, and the Guinness yeast, which can trace its ancestors right back to the first Arthur Guinness, is no exception. It gets very upset in the presence of foreign bodies called 'wild yeasts' which can float undisciplined in the air. Yeast has to be carefully protected against infection of any kind. In short, as a living organism, yeast has to be kept happy if it is to do its job efficiently and there is a story (which I want to believe) that the member of the laboratory staff who was the yeast minder has been known to come into the laboratory on Christmas Day just to make sure the yeast is not unhappy or feeling left out or neglected. The job that yeast has to do is to convert the hopped wort into alcohol, and carbon dioxide.

That done, and given several days maturation, we have that magic liquid Guinness stout.

There used to be, and may still be, a theory that there was a secret ingredient in Guinness. A second theory said that the secret lay in the right mixture of the right raw materials. Another theory said that there was no secret ingredient but a secret way of brewing which was all about temperatures and length of time at various stages of the process and so on. It has often been said that only brewers in Guinness knew these secrets, and that brewers were sworn to secrecy on oath at some kind of clandestine midnight induction ceremony.

little docket called a 'scrip'. This was a ticket that entitled the holder to an extra one or two pints of Guinness at one of the 'taps' in the Brewery. It was given in cases where an employee would do something special over and above his duties. In the eyes of the other ranks that power to sign a scrip was positively awesome and the recipient of a scrip was a very lucky man indeed.

No. 2 Staff

Next down the Guinness hierarchy was the No. 2 Staff and, while almost all commissioned ranks above this were Protestants, from now on downwards they were almost all Catholics. This rank was a mixture of people from within and without the organisation who passed an exam at the age of twenty-one. For those inside, it was the last opportunity to get a commission to the No. 2 Staff; otherwise one was destined for a life-long career among 'other ranks' – or possibly one would be obliged to leave the Company altogether. Outsiders who sat this exam had to be sons of No. 2 Staff members. It was a chance for them to join their dad in the secure world of St James's Gate.

This rank had a dining room, which they shared with what were known as the 'Lady Clerks'. This was not in any way a misnomer for these administrative and secretarial staff because, in those days, that is exactly what they were – 'ladies' and 'clerks'. They first entered St James's Gate in 1900 and their successors have been there ever since.

Unclassified

After that came a very curious rank indeed. It was a kind of no-man's land. It was a group which were, so to speak, neither commissioned nor non-commissioned. They spent their careers in places like laboratories and the Dispensary and they inhabited the 'nearly there' world of the warrant officer. They were called 'unclassified'.

FREE BEER

Possibly since 1759, every employee over twenty-one years of age was entitled to have two pints of Guinness, free of charge, every working day. At the Guinness Brewery there were several distribution points where the men went, twice a day, and had a pint served to them in strong aluminium tankards.

Appropriately enough, these points were known as 'taps'. As someone involved in communications for most of my life, it strikes me that those Brewery taps were a splendid source of Brewery information and gossip and rumour – just the kind of things that most people thrive on – talk about who was on the sick list or on holidays, who had been promoted or transferred, who had retired, married or died, who had had an increase in family, had had a sports achievements, who had performed well or not so well in the Company.

If an employee was a teetotaller or just not interested in drinking these two daily pints, the Company said to itself that it was hardly fair to give some people a daily gift of two pints and give nothing to those who did not wish to avail of this particular gift. So they worked out a system of allowing the non-drinker two pence for every pint he could have had, but elected not to have. At that time,

Continued on page 27

There will be a pint with the author for the best suggestion for a caption to go with this picture!

This was a favourite Guinness horse. His drayman recorded that 'he learned how to undo the
latch of his stable door with his nose so we had to put a double bolt on it to keep him in'.

Here is another team, in a scene much enhanced by the cobblestone yard.

Two of the Richardson's horses and the Geoghegan engine in the Cooperage Department c 1955

The trace horse in action. When the load on the dray was particularly heavy, or when the journey involved going uphill, a trace horse was harnessed up to the dray to help pull it.

The pride of the Guinness stables. The first team on its way to compete for 'best turned-out trade transport' at the prestigious annual show at the RDS in Ballsbridge. More often than not they won first prize — and no wonder! Even the horse got an extra pint in his mash afterwards.

*The opening of the Grand Canal, which allowed supplies of Guinness to be transported direct by water
to the Guinness stores at Limerick and Ballinasloe, was the start of the Guinness trade spreading all
over the country. The picture, taken c 1950, shows supplies arriving via Richardson's horse drays at the
St James's Gate terminal of the canal for loading on to canal barges.*

*Guinness yeast, progeny of the yeast culture
originally used in 1759, on board an aircraft
on its way to a Guinness brewery overseas*

*Ready for any emergency. The Guinness Fire Brigade men complete with their Merryweather fire engine.
Everything about this unit smacked of discipline, readiness, dedication and challenge.*

Continued from page 18

a pint cost something like nine pence in a pub but the Brewery worked out things like the actual cost of producing a pint and excise duty on it and so on and eventually decided that an allowance of two pence per pint was equitable. And so, at the end of every four weeks, the non-drinker got nearly a pound in his pay packet as what was called 'Beer Money Allowance'. I can never quite get over the principle of an employer paying his employee for not accepting a gift of his product!

Alas, the taps were closed in the 1970s cost-cutting exercise, and the draught stout has been replaced by bottled stout for drinking off the premises.

Employees on the active list were not the only people to get free Guinness. For a long time the Medical Department prescribed Guinness for some of their patients, which was handed out to them in special six-ounce bottles called 'nips'. This was simply following the dictum that Guinness Is Good For You and was doubly useful when 'topping up' tonic drugs that were in short supply during the wars. It made a very good substitute tonic and, according to the medics, often gave much better results! The Company also gave free supplies amounting to six dozen 'nips' of Guinness every week to Dublin hospitals and convalescent homes for medical use.

Employees

And so we move down to the non-commissioned ranks. Members of this order were collectively called 'employees'. Many of them were craftsmen – fitters, carpenters, plumbers, electricians, boilermakers and so on, whose job it was to maintain all plant, machinery and premises within St James's Gate. In the 1930s there were some five hundred craftsmen working in the Brewery.

The Trades Group

The craftsmen – or 'Trades Group' – had their own system of seniority starting with apprentices and ending up with foremen and supervisors. Most of these trades had guilds going back a very long time and they reserved the right to dictate the terms of entry and the work practices of their members. They also organised their own training of apprentices and the supervision of their work. In short, the 'Trades' had a very effective 'closed shop' system and, in the main, apprentices tended to be sons of tradesmen. Whatever else can be said about that system it certainly worked well.

Labourers

The biggest group at St James's Gate was the class of general labourer, whose work was supervised by foremen. The easiest way to describe what they did is to say that they did everything nobody else did. They kept the place clean and polished; they washed and filled casks; drove lorries; loaded rail wagons and barges; delivered Guinness to pubs; took back empty casks; acted as security guards at Brewery gates – and so on, *ad infinitum*. Most of them wore dungarees and boots, or other attire suitable for their work, supplied free of charge. Many of them had entered the Brewery at fourteen years of age and they went on pension when they reached sixty-five.

They worked a five-and-a-half-day week and, at one time, their days off amounted to all Sundays, Good Friday, Christmas Day, Whit Monday, the first Monday in August and one other day called 'Annual Leave Day'.

Lads and boys

Male employees between the ages of fourteen and eighteen were officially classified as 'boys'. You could get a job as a laboratory attendant, boy messenger, boy labourer, or telephone exchange operator. And, whatever the job, you got a free issue of suitable clothes to go with it – even to the extent that the uniformed boys on the switchboard had leather patches beautifully sown into the elbows of their jacket and a strip of leather likewise put into their sleeve ends because, with a lot of desk work, their uniforms would have been quickly worn out without these additions.

Once a 'boy' reached eighteen, he became what was officially classified as a 'lad' and transferred to other work. Some lads did labouring work of one kind or another; most became what was known as 'number-takers'. Most important, lads' wages were three pounds and ten shillings, quite a lot more than 'boys' earned.

They remained lads until they reached the age of twenty-one, at which stage they usually went on to become labourers. However, there was no guarantee of this. In fact when we reached the age of eighteen we were obliged to sign a form acknowledging that, on reaching twenty-one years of age 'my services will then be dispensed with and I shall have no claim to another appointment or to any compensation or gratuity on leaving the service'.

And there, at least for the present, I'm leaving the categorisation of Guinness personnel as it existed in 1938 and for heaven knows how many decades before that. I know I'm leaving out small pockets of people here and there (like the crews who manned the Guinness ships which sailed from Dublin to Liverpool and Manchester) but I have to draw the line somewhere – and I'm almost there.

Life at the Bottom

When I joined the Company as a boy messenger my obedience and respect went almost entirely to my boss – a member of another classification called 'men messengers'. Almost all of this rank were ex-British Army World War I soldiers. Some wore messenger uniforms like the boy messengers, but others wore a livery of dark serge pants with a red stripe down the sides of the pants, a starched fly-collar and tie, a very smart 'tails' jacket of a maroon hue with brass buttons, and black shoes so shined as to double for a mirror. These old warriors proudly displayed their war ribbons over the top left pocket. As you might imagine, their uniforms and shoes were impeccably kept, with their brass buttons shining like jewels.

In turn, they demanded the same spit and polish from their troops – the boy messengers. And the man in charge of our little platoon carried out an inspection every morning before we were allowed to go into action. Since we were supplied free of charge with Brasso, Cherry Blossom boot polish and a set of brushes, we had no excuse for not being smart. These men had been through hell – the Dardanelles, the Somme, Ypres – and, like most men who had survived, they had a soft underbelly despite their sergeant-major, battle-scarred exterior. They treated each day as another bonus.

Answering the bell

To come back to my boss, my mentor Butcher, my three other mates in our unit and my first day at work. One of

29

the first things I learned was that I had to say 'sir' to every gentleman in every office in the building and 'miss' to every Lady Clerk.

Next, I had to sit on a long and too high (my feet couldn't reach the floor) bench in the hall of No. 1 Thomas St. On the wall over our heads was an array of little circles with a number on each and a bell sitting over all. These were connected up with the offices and when the bell rang you did two things. You checked which number was ringing and then you scurried as fast as you could to the office that rang. There you were given a letter or a book or some such and told where to deliver it. For the first day or two I trailed alongside Butcher and began to know what things were about and where places were.

One thing was certain. If No. 7 bell rang I was never, ever to answer it. The reason was that No. 7 was the Head Brewer's office and only my boss was qualified or allowed to serve this personage. For an untouchable to enter pukka sahib's quarters while he was in them was a heinous crime.

The Brewery postal system

Butcher introduced me to my duties one by one. It started with the Brewery postal system. Almost every office in the Company had its little tin post-box on the wall just inside the door. And every hour the boy messenger attached to a particular office block did the rounds of the offices collecting and delivering letters.

When we got back down to our station we put the letters we collected into a large box and, every hour, a post boy came from the Guinness Post Office HQ. He collected what we had collected from our offices and he delivered what he had for our block. We sorted the incoming mail and distributed it. Our building was six storeys high. There was a lift, but messengers were not allowed to use it if a lady or gentleman was using it or waiting to use it, so we kept very fit.

The post boys who called on us on the hour went off back to their HQ in the Brewery Post Office. This was a hub of excitement. It was like Piccadilly Circus with so many uniformed boys dumping their incoming loads, taking a ten-minute breather, filling up their post-bag with more stuff and setting off again on their trip around the sixty-four-acre site. Meantime, the boys who worked as sorters sat at a very large table opposite a set of pigeon-holes and flung the letters into wherever they should be flung. In came letters both from internal sources and from the outside world. And out went letters to Brewery destinations and to the outside world.

This last bit intrigued me because it was the first time I had seen a franking machine in operation. I thought it was pure magic. So this whole Guinness Post Office system was no more or less than a miniature version of the large public post office and sorting station across the road in James's Street. The Guinness postal system employed some twenty boys to do the job and, apart from one or two men in charge of the operation, the rest were all between the ages of fourteen and eighteen.

The Brewery cats

Meantime, at our station, there were many other jobs for us to do apart from jumping into action when the bells rang. We often had to take a ledger or urgent letter to another part of the site. We might have to go down the road to buy cigarettes for 'sirs'. Or if, like me, you were the junior boy, you had to feed the Brewery cats. One of the things you can't allow in a brewery is mice. They can get up to all kinds of mischief like gnawing their way through sacks of grain, leaving their unsanitary marks in an area where hygiene is extremely important.

And one way of keeping them out is cats. The Brewery cats (there were dozens of them) were so good at their job that there wasn't a mouse to be caught. But cats have to be fed. So every day, at precisely 2.15 in the afternoon, I took a beautifully sterilised, stainless steel bucket to the kitchens in the Catering Department where two important things happened. One was that a chef, an ex-Royal Dublin Fusiliers sergeant with a massive moustache, would sit me down in a corner of the kitchen and give me a huge helping of whatever left-over pudding was on the menu that day in the Directors' dining room.

Well I can tell you I would have fed all the cats in Dublin for the exotic goodies I got. While I was wolfing this down, the bucket was taken away and filled with raw fish the likes of which we at home could never afford. And then off I went on my rounds of St James's Gate and into nooks and crannies never even dreamt of by the vast majority of people who worked there. Whatever about the children following the Pied Piper of Hamlin, the Brewery cats were there to say hello and rub up against me at the same places every day and spot on time. I used to try and have a chat with them but they weren't in the least interested. Why should they be? After all, a fillet of plaice is a fillet of plaice, but some young fella nattering on about something or other is for some other time.

So, for a couple of years, I fed the Guinness cats. They were just like most other creatures in the Brewery – well-fed, spoiled, loyal, comfortable, decent and smug in the knowledge that they'd never have it so good anywhere else. I often wondered afterwards whether there was a pension scheme for Guinness cats.

The cats actually became the subject of one of the sacred Board orders when, out of the boardroom came the edict that 'The authorised establishment of brewery cats must be strictly adhered to.' In due course a copy of this went to the Head Brewer, who passed it down the line to his subordinates with the comment 'Senior Tomcat to note'!

Policing the Brewery

On the cat run I'd see men doing all sorts of jobs. Sometimes I'd see a policeman. Yes, the Company had its own uniformed police force – what today might be called 'security'. There were about six of them and most if not all of them had been sergeants or sergeants-major in the British army. They too wore their medal tabs on their uniforms.

Their job was to patrol the entire premises, night and day, to make sure all was well and, perhaps especially, to ensure that the no-smoking rules were obeyed – if you were caught smoking you were fined heavily – and that there was no pillaging.

Whatever about the other dictionary meanings of that word, 'pillaging' meant only one thing in the Brewery. It meant stealing stout – either by drinking it on the spot or by taking it away to be drunk somewhere else later on. It was – it had to be – a heinous crime and the penalty for conviction was devastating. It was instant suspension from duty, followed by a 'trial' at which the policeman had to produce the evidence and the charged man was given the opportunity to plead innocence or guilt. If found guilty the man was given whatever 'back' pay he was due and then summarily dismissed.

It was a very hard tradition but all agreed that it was necessary. With all that stout lying around in various vessels the temptation to steal could be very strong and only the severest penalty for being caught was enough to deter. In practice, dismissal very rarely happened and, when it did, all those concerned were most upset. Including the policeman involved.

I know this to be true because my father's brother, my uncle Tom, was senior policeman. I can still see him as I went on my 'cat run'. He was a six-footer and, compared to little me, he was a giant. And yet as he and I stopped for chats among the vats, even he was dwarfed by their

PENSIONS AND FUNERALS

The official line on pensions was that, 'as a result of injury causing total incapacity, or old age,' pensions were granted by the Company, after ten years service and 'at the pleasure of the Board' to all employees on the basis of length of service. These pensions were given without any contribution from the employees and were assessed on the basis of one-sixtieth of salary or wages for each year served – up to a maximum of two-thirds of the salary or wage being paid at the time of pension. The ordinary pension age was sixty for ungraded men, sixty-five for graded men and fifty-five for females.

The number of pensioners on the books in 1943 was 849. The average pension paid in that year was fifty-seven shillings a week. Moreover, all pensioners, plus their dependants, plus all widows of ex-Brewery employees, were eligible to continue to avail of all medical and welfare services provided by the Company similar to those they were getting while 'on the active list'. That concession is one still enjoyed today by all 'on the active list' plus their dependants, and all pensioners plus their dependants. It must rank as one of the most beneficial and generous gestures made by any organisation anywhere in the world. And it has been like that for well over a century.

After 'active service' comes pension. And, alas and alack, after pension comes... There once was a Brewery insurance society, known in quirky Dublin humorous terms as the 'Bury Yourself Society'. Employees could regularly pay in small amounts as a saving so that, when the bell tolled, there was a little money available for a funeral. These payments amounted to sixpence a week per adult and a penny a week for children under ten. It was a sad little society but a very practical one and, in the early 1940s, it had just over 1300 members. In those days the average amount drawn out for a funeral was £30 – just about enough for decent obsequies. In addition to the savings by employees the Company gave a 'per funeral' grant of £4.

enormous size. Brewery policemen didn't fraternise with the other men because they were a breed apart. They couldn't be seen to mix with the men because of their declared objectivity in doing their job. So it always gave me a thrill when I met him on my rounds. He was kind and friendly to me and I got some kind of thrill when I knew that some of the men were watching this chat session. I felt I knew people in high places and wasn't just any new boy in the place!

Minding the loos

Other duties we had to perform when the bells weren't ringing was to check the toilet paper and change the linen rollers in the 'gentlemen's' and 'ladies'' toilets in our office block. The rule was that, since we were not allowed to enter the ladies' loo after 8.45 in the mornings because a lady might be in there, we looked after the ladies' loo first. I have to admit that being able to enter these up-to-now forbidden areas of my world gave me an odd thrill.

The linen rollers were changed every day. The soiled ones were collected in the linen basket and we took them to a central office where they were counted out in dozens and given to the widows of Guinness ex-employees. They took them home, washed and ironed them, and brought them back spick-and-span next day – and got paid for their work. Of course it would have been far easier and probably cheaper to send them off to one of the local laundries, but the Company took the opportunity for Guinness widows to earn some extra money besides their pension. It was strictly optional but many's the widow who was happy to take advantage of yet another illustration that the Company cared for what was known as the Guinness Family.

In the same way the Company offered additional, optional work as office cleaners to any Guinness widows who wanted it. The result was that quite an army of Brewery widows turned up at six o'clock each morning and left again three hours later. No wonder it was said of Guinness that it was a job 'from womb to tomb'! Many of these women were picked up by a small fleet of Guinness transport which went north and south of the Liffey and brought them to work by 6am. Armed with buckets and pails, brushes and mops, vacuum and polishing machines they attacked four hundred offices each working morning and left them spick and span by 9am.

The lavatories, like the people who used them, were catergorised partly by sex and partly by a strict awareness of, and adherence to, hierarchical structures in St James's Gate in those days. The classification by sex was easy. Women were women and, apart from boy messengers changing roller towels, only women could enter a lavatory marked 'Ladies'.

In the case of men, it was more difficult and followed the rank structure from Board members down to messenger boys, from High Command to rookie privates. It was just after my training-period uncoupling from Butcher that an incident happened which shook me for some time. Messengers could use the lavatory at their own base camp. And they were also allowed to use any of the several men's lavatories at various points on the site. So the day came when I found myself in one of the brewing areas and in need of a lavatory. I watched the men heading for the loo and dallied a while to find out what the routine was. There were turnstiles and a little office strategically placed so that the man inside the window of the office was in control of the turnstiles. As each man pushed his way through the turnstile he shouted his number to the loo guardian who made a note of it in a ledger and pushed a few sheets of loo paper under the glass so that the man took the paper and went in to find a vacancy. Easy, thought I.

WAGES AND BENEFITS

One of the many reasons why a job in the Guinness Brewery was looked on as 'the tops' was because of the way the Company looked after its employees. Another reason was the comparatively high rates of pay. During World War II, the average gross wages paid to all labourers in the Company was eighty-eight shillings (four pounds eight shillings) a week. Hours of work were forty-four per week – 8am to 5pm with an hour for dinner, Monday to Friday, and 8am to noon on Saturday, unless of course you were on shift work.

If an employee was convalescing from illness, the Company often paid his rail fare to a country cousin or seaside resort and also allowed him full pay during his stay there. When an employee of labouring or tradesman status was on the 'sick list' his wages stopped and what was known as 'sick pay' came into operation. This was a combination of payments via the National Health Insurance Act plus what the Company paid. Totals for the employee amounted to the following:

Married Men (if at home) – 75% of wages; (if in hospital) – 66% of wages

Single Men (if at home) – 50% of wages; (if in hospital) – 25% of wages

Full pay was granted, however, for compulsory absence due to infectious disease (which meant the employee was in quarantine) and also for absence arising from vaccination. There was also a rule which said that 'Full pay may be granted in exceptional cases such as large family, prolonged illness entailing extra expense etc.' Full pay was also given in the case of people slowly dying from cancer or some such incurable disease.

All men were entitled to an annual holiday of six days with full pay. In addition he was given an 'excursion allowance' of thirty shillings, plus five shillings for each child under fourteen. For some inexplicable reason the 'excursion allowance' for unmarried men was only twenty-five shillings.

The excursion was often taken in the form of what the bus company in those days called a 'Mystery Tour'. This meant that you turned up at the bus terminal with wife, plus children, plus Guinness voucher worth thirty shillings in your hand and you went off on a bus tour lasting four hours and stopping off at a series of interesting places within about fifty miles of Dublin. The 'mystery' part was that only the driver knew where he was going and he was sworn to silence on the matter.

So I went through the observed routine, shouted my number, collected my paper ration and sought a stall. The trouble was that, in my case, my requirements were very simple – just a urinal. I found one, used it, felt better and prepared to leave. That's when the problem presented itself. What to do with the unused loo paper? Easy. Honesty is the best policy. Give it back to the man. I did. But he stopped me in my tracks. Why was I returning the paper? Because I didn't require it. But did I not give my number on entering? Yes. Then I shouldn't have done that, said the man: 'You only give your number if you require lavatory paper.' Then he put that statement into words which I have carried with me throughout life. He said, simply, 'Peeing doesn't count.' Well. It was my first official reprimand from a Brewery 'official' and it was the first time I had to consider this matter of bodily functions in an entirely new light. What a milestone that day was!

Incidentally, I have never been able to work out why the Brewery lavatories for 'other ranks' required a custodian in an office with a duty to check on who was using the facilities within his bailiwick. Some said that, at the end of the day, he added up the list of all those numbered men who had, so to speak, left their business with him and, from that, he could work out the total of what might be called 'down time'. If all non-staff lavatories in the Brewery did the same thing, then Guinness would know the total 'down time' per day and, said the pundits, the Company could claim back money from the Revenue Commissioners or some such to pay for work not done – if you follow me. But another guru said that the system was installed to prevent laggards from over-use of the toilet instead of being at their work.

One last word about this immensely interesting subject. The title given by the men to the custodian of the loo was 'jakes clerk'. I presume it was a pensionable post and I often wonder what occupation a pensioned Guinness jakes clerk could pursue as a second career.

The life of a messenger

After a few days of 'twinning' with Butcher, I was sent off into town to be measured for my messenger uniform. I thought I'd never get my hands on it. Two fittings and a week later and there was this spanking new suit complete with my first pair of long pants! Pants, jacket with buttoned-up mandarin collar, new boots, a pill-box cap complete with peak and the best raincoat I've ever owned. And all free! I thought I was the smartest thing in the world!

As boys, we were each entitled to a free lunch every day. It was officially described as 'a substantial meat lunch'. And so indeed it was. Soup, meat and potatoes and vegetable, pudding and a choice of milk or orange juice. We were allowed half an hour from arrival at the lunchroom to departure from it and back to base. We were supervised by the men messengers who sat at top table and kept an eye on this mixture of jostling, mischief-making sprogs as if we were all in a barrack mess. But it was a midday break for us and, in more ways than one, we felt better after lunch.

Normally we started work at 8.45am and finished at 4.30pm. Just outside the Brewery back gate there was a building called the 'Workmen's Rooms'. It was where the lads and the men went for their subsidised lunch. It also had a large room with about six private bathrooms which were for free use by any employee. At 4.30 these were mostly not in use and many a boy went and had a luxurious bath – complete with towel and soap – all for nothing.

Also in the Workmen's Rooms there were two billiards tables and we organised and ran many an exciting snooker competition, with prize money amounting to the enormous sum of a pound. At Christmas things reached dizzy heights because, in many office blocks and departments, the staff would do a whip-round for boy messengers and we might easily end up with several pounds in our pockets. It often amounted to a few weeks' wages so the excitement was wonderful. The prize fund for snooker might reach the one-pound-ten-shilling or even the two-pound mark!

Now that I was in uniform, I was allowed to enter the offices occupied by the Head Brewer and what was known as the Second Brewer. Once inside the panjandrum's sanctuary, our job was straightforward enough. We were not to touch anything except... and I'll take them one by one. We extracted the blotting paper from the blotting pad and replaced it with a piece of virginal white blotting paper. The fact that there wasn't a mark on the piece already there was not our business – although, brought up as I was to waste-not-want-not, it hurt me to see this unnecessary and wasteful morning exercise. But ours was not to reason why.

Next we checked the levels in both the red and black ink pots. In the absence of an inkpot equivalent of the Plimsoll line, we were nevertheless expected to keep the levels 'just right'. That done, we had to make sure that the nibs in the pens were wiped clean and in proper order for the onerous day's work ahead. And lastly, we had to change the calendars. One calendar hung on the wall and showed three months at a time – the previous, the present and the next month – and had a small, square cursor which you moved along a perspex band and brought to rest on the day that was in it. The other calendar, which sat on a corner of the magisterial desk, was a box-like item about six by four inches, made of lovely wood and with three apertures facing the regal chair. The top slit showed the month, the bottom slit showed the day and the large centre one showed the date of the month. To change these you twiddled little knobs on the side of the box. I loved that little box. But there was one thing that bothered me about it. I couldn't work out why this nawab didn't change it himself instead of employing us to do it for him. Perhaps this was my first opaque glimpse of the need to cut costs.

I've mentioned that St James's Gate had its own staff of tradesmen – electricians, plumbers and so on. They each had their own base – it was called their 'shop', the plumbers' shop for example. Each shop was a hive of activity and full of noise. It was where the craftsmen had all their tools and equipment and benches at which they did their work. There was singing and whistling and banging and shouting. All very exciting for a young boy of fourteen and, as I learned, it was young greenhorns like me who often gave them a good laugh. The procedure was simple. One of the senior boys in our unit told me one day to go over at once to the plumbers' shop and ask one of the plumbers for a bucket of steam and bring it back to our base. Dutiful as ever, off I went to the shop unaware of the fact that the foreman of the shop had been tipped off by phone that young Byrne was on his way over 'for the usual'.

As I entered the shop I was greeted by the foreman. 'What can I get you, sonny?' Oliver Twist-like I explained my requirements. Certainly. We'll do that for you. Then he pointed to a man at a bench and when I got to him he gave me an empty bucket and sent me off to another man at another bench to have it filled with steam. 'The usual' was now in motion. I was sent from one plumber to another all of whom were 'out of steam today'. I then noticed that each plumber had lined up behind me as I went on my search for steam until, eventually, most of the plumbers were standing around me laughing their heads off and clapping. The penny dropped. All a joke. Was my face red! But the great thing was that they all enjoyed the harmless bit of fun and the foreman clinched the deal by giving me a tanner as I left. All good, clean fun.

So gullible was I that, a few weeks later, I was sent off

to the electricians' shop to collect a 'wimwam for a woegee' and bring it back to my boss. The same routine and the same fun. And both occasions looking for something which didn't exist. Learning a little about lifemanship? Certainly learning about initiation rites in Guinness.

Continuing education

The Company had a free education programme for boys and lads. Although it was not obligatory to avail oneself of the scheme, the Company took a poor view of boys or lads who did not continue their education by attending evening classes at a technical college (or 'tech'). Briefly, we could elect to attend all or any of the courses which ran from seven until ten, five nights a week, for about eight months of the year. There were all the usual school subjects plus additional ones like commerce, book-keeping and accountancy. You could sign on for as many as you liked – but there was a catch. Because your fees were paid direct by Guinness to the colleges, they were happy to supply Guinness with a quarterly attendance return which showed all the sessions you should have attended and all the sessions you actually attended. Where there was a substantial gap between these two figures, you were asked by the Company to explain. Consistently bad performances risked a withdrawal of your tech fees. Not only might you lose the fees but you might also lose your parents' consent to allow you out at night time, which was far more serious from our point of view.

MONEY MATTERS

In addition to providing benefits like free education, the company also acted as banker to its staff. Loans were available to employees who were in trouble with debts, arrears of rent, furnishing new homes etc. A man could borrow up to £10 (£250 in today's money) which was repayable, interest free, at a shilling a week for each one pound borrowed. Payment of a loan was automatically deducted from wages. In 1942, 137 loans amounting to £624 for 'domestic reasons' and £220 for dentures were granted.

The Company also tried hard to get employees to save money. They produced a scheme whereby the men were encouraged to save a shilling a week in the Brewery Savings Bank, and they offered to pay 5% gross interest on whatever was saved.

Employees of Guinness also had their own lending institution, the Guinness Permanent Building Society or GPBS, founded in 1901. Its declared objective at the time of its foundation was 'to provide finance by way of loans to members of the brewery to purchase their first modest dwelling house'. The society was administered by a committee of twelve volunteers drawn from all ranks and all levels of the Brewery working community. Apart from that, Company personnel were used to attend to the day-to-day administrative work of the society, including staff in the Accountants Department and Personnel Department. Between carrying the costs of this administrative help, plus direct subsidies to the society, the Company has given support worth about £1m.

From 1901 to 1982 the society provided £3,756,000 (over £90m in today's money) in over 1584 separate loans. And all of this money was spent by the GPBS as mortgages required by Guinness personnel borrowers to enable them to buy houses or apartments. The value of the loans amounted to between 90% and 95% of the value of the property being bought.

Most of the money lent by the GPBS came in via investments made by members of the society. These investments were made in cash or by routine deduction from wages and salaries. The interest paid out on such investments was at least equal to what other building societies paid and it was free of standard rate income tax. The borrowing rate was about 1.5% less than that on offer from any other building society. One reason why that benefit was available was because of the Company's gesture in carrying some of the costs of running the society.

Come April of each year, you sat an examination in your subjects. This exam was run by the government's Department of Education who marked the papers and sent results to Guinness. If you did outstandingly badly you were cautioned about possible withdrawal of fees. But if you did particularly well the Company rewarded you with cash prizes. Some did very well on this and you could earn up to £15 for a really good performance. It also meant that, when you reached eighteen, you could sit the Leaving Certificate exam on an almost level pegging with the kids who had remained at school.

Possession of the Leaving Certificate could open the door to employment outside Guinness and thus avoid the period between the ages of eighteen and twenty-one as a number-taker, followed by a lifetime as a labourer. And, of course, this continuing education improved your hopes of passing the examination for No. 2 Staff appointments when you reached twenty-one.

The rationale behind this education scheme for young employees was simple from Guiness's point of view. Things that helped to make and keep employees contented was good for the employees and good for the Company.

Loans were also made available to all personnel at St James's Gate to assist in meeting the costs of education for their children at school or university or college. These loans were available at the astonishingly low interest rate of one per cent per annum. The Company was prepared to grant loans to cover up to half of the fees for each year, provided the parent paid the other half. Repayment of these loans did not begin until the child's education was completed. But, even then, it could be deferred if there were other children in the family still at school or university. The limit of completion of repayment was before the parent reached normal retirement age.

Other goodies available included bursaries for children of personnel in cases where the child would qualify for a scholarship on the results of an examination, but was excluded because of the operation of a means test. Finally, there were grants available towards the cost of travel to and from school or university in the UK by children of personnel who lived in Ireland. (Why does the word 'nanny' occur to me?)

Meantime I was now fifteen and beginning to know the ropes. My wages had gone up by a shilling a week. I was attending night classes on four nights a week. I was allowed to stay out until after ten o'clock at night – including the nights I was not at the tech. I was allowed to play snooker in the Workmen's Rooms. And I was being well fed and clothed by the Company.

Guinness Colour

The Guinness company was widely known to Dubliners who didn't work for it as well as to those who did, and not just because of the product. Guinness horses and barges, for example, were well-known sights in the city streets.

Horses

When the Brewery was established in 1759, horses and drays were the only means of transporting raw materials into St James's Gate, fulls out to customers, and empties back for washing. Come to think of it, that's not entirely true. There was also the wheelbarrow, which was used for taking a firkin from the Brewery to some nearby pubs. Indeed some say that a pram was often used and I'd like to think that that's true. In any case horses and drays were transporting Guinness from 1759 right up to September 1960 – just over two centuries.

Initially Guinness owned its own fleet of horses. They were housed comfortably at St James's Gate, well-fed and watered, and had a vet to care for them when they weren't feeling well. The ration of Guinness in their daily mash helped keep them in good shape. In 1891 Guinness had 150 horses. In addition, they hired extra ones on busy days from a local Dublin firm called Richardson. With the advent of motor transport, Guinness decided to sell off its horses and, on 6 July 1932, its remaining thirty beauties were pensioned off and the stables closed. But the 1874 contract with Richardson's remained intact and Richardson's horses were still in use right up to 1960. Towards the end of their Guinness work more than half of Richardson's horses were used to transport fulls to the terminal basin of the Grand Canal at the back of St James's Gate. From there the barge set off on its six-day trip to the Guinness store in Limerick. The canal was closed in 1960 and that also saw the close of the 201 years of horse transport at St James's Gate.

We lived on the South Circular Road at Rialto and Richardson's had their stables about half a mile away on Herberton Road. The work of Richardson's horses and draymen for Guinness was done from about 6am to 6pm, six days a week. The men arrived at the stables shortly after 5am, woke up the horses and harnessed them, yoked up the dray, and then set off for one of the loading bays at the Brewery. The route took them down Herberton Road, turn right into South Circular Road, turn left into Rialto Street. When you reached the Grand Canal you turned right and more or less kept going until you reached your loading bay inside the Brewery.

As tiny chisellers, we often woke suddenly in what seemed like the middle of the night to the sound of Richardson's horses clip-clopping their solid way down the South Circular Road. It seemed to us that there were hundreds of them, and they were out in all weathers. The racket was fierce. Small wonder, for these horses were the finest of Clydesdales, Percherons and Shire breeds. They were proud of their handsome, dependable appearance and well they might be.

In contrast to the horses were the draymen, who almost always looked cold, a little underfed and not all that well protected from the weather. But they were invariably cheerful and happy with their horses and glad to have a job when many another was not so lucky.

Like the Guinness barges on the River Liffey, Guinness's horses were a well-known and well-loved part of Dublin life. They were very adept at manoeuvring their way down Molly Malone's 'streets broad and narrow' to deliver the Goodness into back yards or side entrances of pubs instead of cluttering up a main thoroughfare with their bulk. At busy times like Christmas there might be as many as forty horses working the Dublin pubs. Many Dubliners stopped to have a little chat with them, to give them a little something to eat, to rub their noses and generally to keep in touch with such charming old friends.

A sight cherished by Dubliners was a convoy of eight or ten fully loaded drays setting off at 6am from the Brewery and clip-clopping their way along the main road to Bray, a distance of some twelve miles. In Bray, they would off-load their fulls, collect their empties, feed horses and team, and clip-clop their way back to the Brewery by gaslight.

The work entailed long hours on duty for the team on each dray. Depending on the size (and therefore the weight) of casks being delivered there could be two or three men on a dray's team. Apart from the heavy work of lifting casks on and off the dray and lowering them into

Continued on page 59

*The Cash Office at St James's Gate where customers came
to order supplies, to pay their bills and to have their queries settled.
It is easy to see why this office was used in the making of several films*

From 6am to 9am, five mornings a week,
a team of Guinness women set to with mops and brushes, dusters and polish to
clean up the Brewery's offices. These jobs were available to widows of deceased employees
who wanted to augment their widows' pensions with some extra income.

The seat of power. Twin chimneys of the Guinness powerhouse in James's Street can be seen from quite far away. Under-production of energy resulted in connection to the national Electricity Supply Board for requirements, whilst over-production resulted in selling the excess to the national grid.

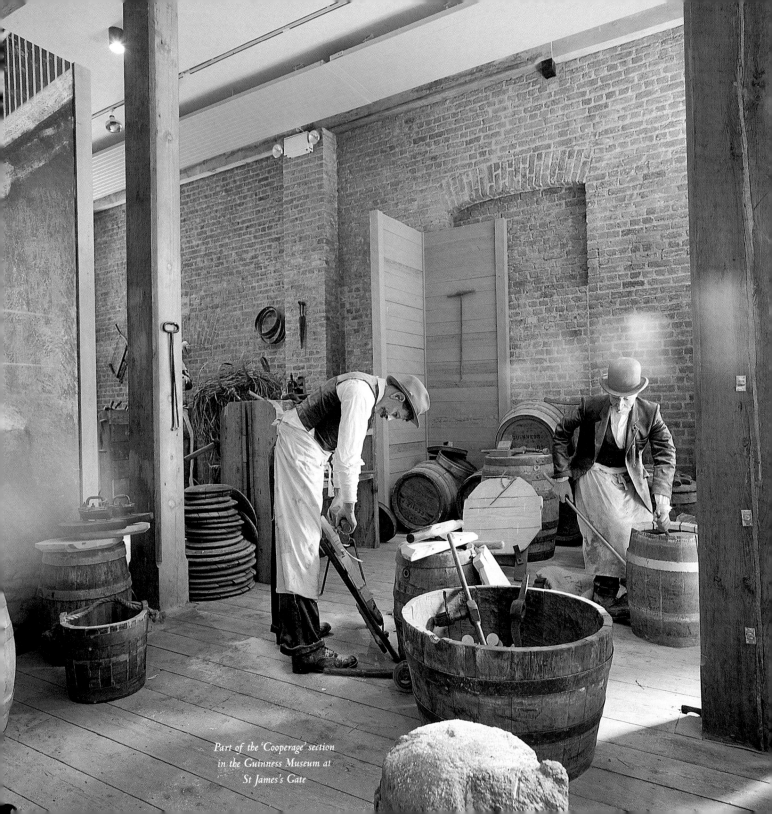

*Part of the 'Cooperage' section
in the Guinness Museum at
St James's Gate*

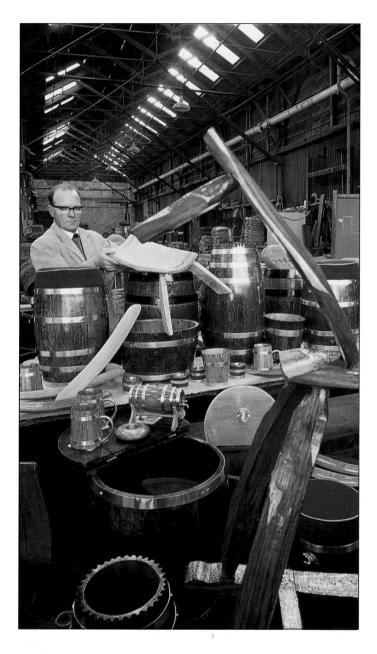

With the end of the wooden casks, the coopers set about using up the stocks of beautiful white oak by making all kinds of furniture such as tables, chairs, stools, ash-trays, mugs, flower-pots, which were sold all over the world.

The fulls have been loaded from barge to ship and the empties from ship to barge. The ship will sail eastwards to Manchester and the barges westwards to the Brewery. The onlooker probably repairs to the nearest pub.

The Lady Grania *in reflective mood on a quiescent Anna Livia Plurabelle*

The Lady Gwendolen *ready to receive its cargo of transportable tanks*

Taking part in a week of celebrations in the city,
The Miranda Guinness *sails past Blackrock, Co Cork.*

*Delivering Guinness to
pubs on the Aran Islands*

The swimming pool in the Bicentenary Centre at St James's Gate. By design it was built a few feet short of Olympic standards to avoid meeting requests for its use by non-Guinness personnel.

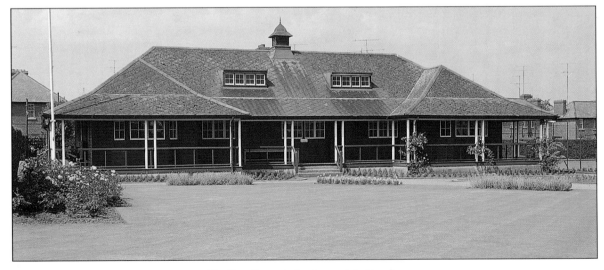

The old pavilion at the Iveagh grounds in Crumlin

One of the fleet of Emerald Star Lines (ESL) luxury cruisers on the Shannon. ESL proved to be one of the Company's diversification successes.

Guinness and all that jazz

The Geoghegan loco. Designed by the chief engineer (1874-1901) at St James's Gate to run on his narrow-gauge (1ft, 10in) railway system for transporting goods throughout the plant. Later he completed the job by designing a method whereby this loco could also run on the broad-gauge (5ft, 3ins) rails. The loco in this picture is on view at the Guinness Museum in St James's Gate.

The secrets of Guinness.. Barley, hops, yeast, water, and a DIY book on
The Theory and Practice of Brewing. *All that's required now is a brewery!*

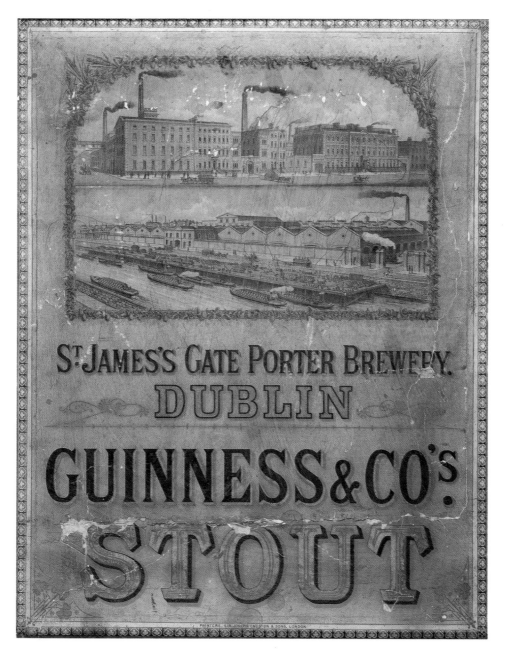

One of the very earliest pieces of showcard advertising for display in Irish pubs.
Modern versions of these showcards are still on display as mirrors in some Irish pubs today.

*A selection of
bottle tops used
in the early
thirties*

Continued from page 42

the pub cellars these men had to be good at PR. They didn't call it that in those days, but that's what it was. They represented Guinness out there in the market place where diplomacy, politeness and good manners were important. They had to try and ensure that neither they nor their impedimenta constituted an accident or injury hazard to any member of the public, so they kept an eagle eye on such potential dangers as open cellar gratings, ropes, dumping pads (called 'bosses') and so on. And they had to ensure that the horse was not becoming involved with passers-by by way of tossing a mane at them – however friendly the gesture. So a constant stream of carefully chosen words and sounds by members of the team was a 'must' if a heavyweight Clydesdale or Percheron felt a bit miffed about something.

Another hazard for the team to overcome was competition for the right parking space outside the pub. True, the situation was nothing as bad as it is today, but still and all a few yards to left or right of the desired parking spot could result in extra work and delays. So the situation required diplomatic handling if an unpleasant altercation was to be avoided.

The same kid-glove handling was advisable when dealing directly with the publican himself. Although he needed and welcomed the delivery, he didn't relish complaints from his customers about any inconvenience caused them as a result of it and neither did he want any whinging from a member of the public about real or imaginary damage or upset caused as a result of the beautiful Shire horse leaving his healthy if unsanitary visiting card on the road. In short, a delivery job was not without its hazards.

Then there was another job these horses were involved in. 'Trace-horses' were used in Dublin's steep streets and lanes to help the drayhorse to pull the load up the hill. (The term 'trace-horse' comes from the two traces or side straps that connect a horse's harness to the dray. When a horse refuses to move in harness he often tries to 'kick over the traces' – hence the expression meaning to break away from control or to run riot.) The trace-horse walked in front of the drayhorse, and his harness, like the harness of the drayhorse itself, was connected to the dray. The idea was to lessen the strain on the drayhorse by sharing the heavy work involved in pulling loads up hills such as encountered in Steevens Lane just outside the Brewery. In fact this particular site of 'tracing' was thought to be the last trace-horse in operation in Ireland.

Depending on the loads they had to draw, the horses sometimes worked in pairs, and in that case they were known as 'pair horses'. Pairs of horses who worked together often had paired names like Pride and Prejudice, Might and Main, Rhyme and Reason or Thunder and Lightning.

Sometimes the horses worked within the Brewery. They were harnessed to bogies on the narrow-gauge railway, or to wagons on the broad-gauge railway, and they moved these from where they were to where they were required to be. It often proved a far easier and less expensive way of shifting rolling-stock than the use of engines.

Guinness horses were frequently entered for competitions at the prestigious Dublin Horse Show, in a category called 'Trade Turn-outs'. One of my uncles, Richard Byrne (whose grandson Finbarr was to become Managing Director of Arthur Guinness Son & Company (Dublin) Ltd), was a Guinness drayman and undoubtedly was often on parade on behalf of the Company at this annual RDS event – hence my particular personal interest in this aspect of the Guinness horses.

At the RDS we saw paraded for all to see the pride of the Guinness drayhorse fleet. It was fully laden with spanking new and unused kilderkins or firkins being pulled by a magnificent Clydesdale brushed to the last and with lacquered hooves and shining shoes plus harness which had been polished to within an inch of its life. And to cap it all were two moustached Guinness draymen beautifully attired in their white corduroy pants, shining black boots, corduroy jacket – and the crowning glory of a hard hat. They sat atop the front row of casks and the whole picture was something not to be forgotten. Small wonder they very often won their event and earned nice trophies, excellent PR for the Company, and of course a pint or two afterwards to celebrate. And, yes, the horse got an extra helping of mash that night.

THE FANCIERS

The term 'fancy' is early-nineteenth-century slang for prize fighters and those involved in the boxing ring sport. It is also sometimes used to describe supporters of other sports and pastimes – especially the breeding of birds and animals. But what on earth could all this have to do with a brewery? Well, if it's the Guinness Brewery, then very few things have nothing to do with it. St James's Gate had the 'fancy'. Or, more correctly called, 'The Fanciers and Industrial Association'. The declared objectives were

> The keeping and breeding of pure bred dogs, poultry, pigeons and cage birds; the cultivation of vegetables and flowers; the encouragement of home industries amongst the families of employees by the holding of an Annual Competition and Exhibition.

At these annual shows thousands of employees, their families and their relatives and friends turned up. Normally the show was held on a Saturday in July. The crowds starting arriving before 2pm. Everyone was in their summer finery. There were stalls displaying all sorts of home-made goodies like cakes, jams and breads. There were displays of photography, dress-making, vegetables, flowers. There were classes arranged exclusively for competitors and exhibitions of wood carving, cage making, fretwork, sketching, cabinet making, handwriting, dancing, darning, children's dresses, hand knitting, plain and fancy sewing, blouse and hat making.

There was a cut-and-style competition for the ladies. There were competitions for best poultry, dogs, pigeons and caged birds. The band played throughout and there was dancing and ballad singing. There was a display of furniture by the Guinness coopers. There were refreshments, and you can guess what that included. It was always the talk of the Company for weeks before and after the event and personnel of all ranks attended and took part.

Inland waterways

Because of the nature of the product that is produced at St James's Gate it is small wonder that water plays such a crucial role in its production. Water is, by bulk, the main ingredient of stout. Water is also essential in keeping the plant and all its brewing vessels and containers clean and sterile. And then, when the product is ready for the marketplace, water again plays a most important part in its transportation and distribution to watering holes far and near. For almost ninety years, it was the water of the Liffey that carried barge loads of Guinness from St James's Gate

to the port of Dublin and, from there, it was and is the Irish Sea water which is the start of journeys which carries the goodness to world markets.

Here in Ireland it was water that first allowed the Brewery to spread its goodness from Dublin to various parts of Ireland by using both of those marvellous inland waterways – the River Shannon and the canals. The oldest known canal system dates back to 5000 BC (in 1968 archaeologists tracked the remains of one of this age in Iraq), and records show that it was the Chinese who invented locks – and that goes as far back as AD 980. It seems that canals were a winner from the start, when some clever fellow showed that a horse drawing a wagon on a roadway could move less than two tons even on short journeys, whereas on a canal, a single horse could fairly easily pull a barge with a load weighing 50 tons.

One of the original and major reasons why Guinness took to using the canal was because of the atrocious condition of the Irish roads at that time. They were often little better than dirt tracks – especially in winter. In periods of bad weather the ruts in them were so deep that travellers could be hidden from view and there were potholes where a man might drown on a dark night. There was no coherent system of road building or road maintenance nor any structured bodies such as local authorities charged with this responsibility. All of which meant that it would have been impossible to transport Guinness by road if for no other reason than that the casks would not have coped with the jolting and battering. So with roads not being suitable, and the railways not yet available (they came fifty years after the waterways), the Grand Canal was the only effective means in those years of transporting Guinness from Dublin to country areas.

The construction of the Grand Canal was started in 1756. It is the longest canal in Ireland or in the UK. When it eventually broke into the Shannon at Shannon Harbour in 1804 it was eighty-two miles long. From there you crossed the Shannon and ended up via Limerick in the Atlantic Ocean. That meant that you could travel by waterway from the Irish Sea to the Atlantic Ocean – which made it the longest system of inland navigation in the British Isles. These canals in Ireland were extremely well built. They had harbours, quays and extensive storehouses at all the main points along the way. At one stage there were waterside hotels for passengers. Apart from any of the other advantages which the Grand Canal brought to Ireland it certainly was a major incentive and opportunity for Guinness to extend its Irish market from the Dublin area to most parts of Ireland.

Coming into James's Street harbour the canal barges were laden with malted barley collected from the major malt-houses which were on the Grand Canal system. When they left again they were full to the gunwhales with casks of Guinness and heading for Guinness stores in Limerick, Ballinasloe (the first Guinness store in Ireland), Carrick-on-Shannon and other places.

But it wasn't only Guinness who used the Grand Canal as its means of transport. These barges also carried wheat and whiskey, sugar and salt, turf and coal, farm produce – and of course people. Passengers were well looked after. Rules for travelling by barge included:

- No servant in livery to be admitted to the 1st Class cabins.
- Dogs and cats in cabins to be paid for like passengers.
- No gaming on Sundays under penalty of 2 guineas for each offence to the Master of the boat.
- No wine to be sold to passengers in the 2nd class cabin

(No mention of Guinness for anybody!)

There was a time when these canal barges were pulled along by horses plodding their comatose way along the narrow strip of grass by the water's edge. They were led along by an equally comatose member of the crew holding the bridle with his butty standing on the deck, hand on tiller, and steering. When they got to a bridge everything stopped, because the strip of grass ran out under the bridge. The horse was unyoked and led up on to the road, across the bridge, and back down to grassland at the other side. The rope was thrown to the captain who tied it to the deck and off they sailed (if that is the correct word) to the next bridge.

As a child I watched this highly complex procedure

many times. As kids living near the canal we had to become involved. We were allowed to throw the rope back to the captain or even help to lead the docile horse from one side of the canal bridge to the other. When we felt particularly bold we recited the ditty which was well-known to the bargemen and always (well, nearly always) elicited a laugh from them:

> Full steam ahead, the captain cried
> For we are sorely pressed
> The chief engineer on the bank replied
> The horse is doing its best.

When the barges became mechanised, the trip from St James's Gate to the Guinness store in Limerick took between four and seven days depending on season and weather. One can only guess at the time taken from Dublin to Shannon Harbour when they were horse-drawn. But by horse or by engine the casks of stout remained below the water level for the entire journey and this meant a steady ambient temperature in the hold. By the time the Guinness reached its destination it was in ideal condition for consumption and there's many a seasoned Guinness drinker who will swear that he could always tell a pint of Guinness which had travelled to him via water as against one which had travelled by road.

As if to fulfil a self-imposed and almost sacred duty of making sure that their cargo was improving while under their responsibility it was common knowledge that some of these bargemen were known to sample the product as they sailed along. Emulating the best of the coopers' craft they could bore a hole in a wooden cask, draw off whatever quantity of Guinness they required to sample it thoroughly, insert a spike into the hole, seal it off by hammering it home, and proceed to sample carefully and conscientiously. Any doubts about such crucial factors as flavour, temperature, head retention, after-taste and so on might well justify another sample. Well! Whatever else we may think about this behaviour we can borrow Sean O'Casey's words and say that 'it kept them from the sin of idleness'. And in the long winter nights on the canals of Ireland a little of something you fancy can bring a little solace.

Seasoned mariners maintain that water should always be treated with caution and respect because it is rarely if ever to be trusted. That warning is especially true of the loughs on the River Shannon. They seem to get agitated without warning and suddenly there can be one hell of a blow and swell and very uncomfortable sailing conditions. That's what happened to the Grand Canal Company barge No. 45M.

It happened on Sunday 1 December 1946 when it was on a trip from St James's Gate with a barge-load of Guinness and heading for the Guinness store in Limerick. As per routine it was towed across Lough Derg by the tug-boat *St James*. At Parker's Point, between Portroe and Killaloe (said to be one of the most treacherous parts of the Shannon), they were hit by a fierce gale. The buffeting from the high wind caused the cargo of full casks to shift. The tow-rope snapped. The *St James* could do nothing to help. The barge heeled over and sank. Three members of the 45M were drowned. One man made it to the shore.

When the storm abated and the water calmed there was no trace of 45M or its cargo. It was lying somewhere on the bottom of Lough Derg in 120 feet of water. Twenty-nine years later it was located by a team who set out to bring it to the surface. Using some hundred air-filled drums, a lot of machinery, determination, skill, conquest over bad weather and many many days of very hard work, 45M eventually broke the surface. It was towed to a safe berth. Unfortunately it was not possible for the recovery team to celebrate their great success because 'we could not drink the toast with any of the 1900 gallons of stout in the hold as it had not "matured" during its 29 years under water'. The barge is now restored to its 'as new' condition and came back to 'tut-tut' its way in the waterways of Ireland.

Guinness barges on the Liffey

If, during the first sixty years or so of the twentieth century, any worthwhile Dubliner were asked to recommend the outstanding sights of Dublin to people from other parts of Ireland or, for that matter, from any part of the world the answer was likely to be a list of some six or seven 'musts'. It would surely include Trinity College, O'Connell Street, the Phoenix Park, Merrion and Fitzwilliam Squares, Dublin

GAMBLING AND DRINK

The Guinness Company always took an interest in all aspects of its employees' lives, and in the 1930s, it shared the view that gambling in Ireland replaced drink as 'Public Enemy Number One'. It also shared the view that gambling 'tends to empty a man's pocket and undermines his morale and intellectual strength'.

At that time many weekend soccer matches were played in Dublin before large crowds and although there was far more betting done on English soccer matches there were still quite a few wagers on Dublin soccer. But it was horses and dogs which were the real interests for Irish punters. Ready-money betting was very prevalent and there were many premises licensed as 'bookies', but the Company had good reason to believe that there were some of its employees who ran a little 'lay the odds' on the premises. That was not to be tolerated but it went on all the same.

Drinking was another social matter in which the employer Guinness was involved – apart, that is, from making beer. A survey done in the U K in 1901 (*Poverty, a Study of Town Life* by B. Seebohm Rowntree) said that 'the sum spent by working people on drink is equal to about four-fifths of the sum they spend on rents'. It was assumed that somewhat similar statistics applied to Dublin. That was of interest to Guinness partly because they were producers of drink but also because abuse of it often led to unwanted domestic turmoil for its employees and for the public at large. That was something Guinness wanted to help eradicate or at least reduce.

Came the 1940s and things in Dublin had changed somewhat. There was a substantial reduction in drunkenness and in drinking generally for two main reasons. One was the high cost of booze, including spirits and beer. The other reason was the continued growth in other attractions such as football matches, horse and dog racing, and a marked increase in 'going to the pictures'. Dublin alone boasted no fewer than forty-one cinemas and Dubliners became quite 'picture-minded'. Golf, for those who could afford it, also grew in popularity. And sales of beer just kept growing steadily but surely.

Before World War II, methylated spirits and the dreaded 'Red Biddy' (a highly intoxicating concoction of red wine and methylated spirits) were far too popular. But the war did away with supplies of 'meths' and, happily for many reasons, these alcoholic depth charges ceased to be available. Among other results of this was that addicts among Guinness employees reverted to what was good for them and this improved their health and well-being.

Castle, the Abbey Theatre and one other item which was so familiar to, and loved by, Dubliners – the Guinness barges on the River Liffey.

They were part of the fabric of life in Dublin. They plied their way from the Guinness jetty at St James's Gate to the port of Dublin where they off-loaded their cargoes of full casks of Guinness on to the Guinness ships which then sailed across the Irish Sea to exotic foreign places like Manchester and Liverpool.

These barges were doing this job since 1873 and one of the saddest sights ever seen in Dublin took place at 6pm on Friday 21 June, Midsummer's Day, 1961 when the 80-foot long by seventeen-foot-one-inch wide barge *Castleknock* sailed from the Custom House Quay with a load of empties and slowly made its funereal way up-river to the jetty at St James's Gate. It was the last time Dubliners would see a Guinness barge doing its job on the Liffey. Truly, many a tear was shed and many a story told that night about a part of Dublin that was gone forever.

At one stage the fleet of barges (they were also known as lighters or, as Louis McNeice in his poem 'Dublin' calls them 'the brewery tugs') numbered eighteen. They each had a name (well what better excuse than a christening party to have a pint of you-know-what?). Most were called after Irish rivers like the *Lagan*, the *Shannon*, the *Lee*, the *Dodder*. Some had the name of an area near Dublin like *Castleknock* (if ever you are near St James's Gate pop into the Guinness Museum in the Hop Store and have a look at the lovely model of this particular barge there), *Killiney, Sandyford, Clonsilla*. When full of Guinness each barge carried 300 hogsheads or 124,800 pints. And since, on an average working day, eight barges chugged their way, fully laden, down-river, it's a thirst-quenching thought that Dubliners looked on as almost a million pints (998,400 to be exact) sailed down Anna Livia Plurabelle and off overseas to God knows where. In their eighty-eight years of active service they were responsible for seeing that more than water passed under the Liffey bridges!

There were five crew members on each barge – a skipper, a mate and three ratings. You knew who was skipper because he had a red band on the sleeve of his serge, polo-neck gansey. Because the big ships sailed on the tide from Dublin port, and also because the barges had to sail to suit the tide on the Liffey, they were in action at all hours of the day and night. On the wall opposite the Guinness jetty at Victoria Quay, there were indelible markings to show the skipper the state of the tide down at the port. It was up to him to see that he sailed precisely on time. And quite often the margins were very tight. The trip down-river from jetty to port normally took twenty minutes. With a strong, wintry east wind on your nose, that time could stretch by a few extra minutes. A tolerance of only four minutes was allowed for such an eventuality and several times a barge failed to make it and had to execute a fast reverse manoeuvre to avoid hitting a bridge and save the crew, the barge, the bridge – and the Guinness! These tides often meant leaving

the Brewery at 3am and getting back to home berth very late in the evening. That, in turn, dictated the hours of loading and unloading. And that meant availability of casks and stout at very odd hours indeed.

There are endless stories told about the barges. Like the time during the Civil War in Dublin in 1920–1 when Dublin Castle had to issue passes to Guinness bargemen to allow them to be out during curfew hours. And there was another Civil War incident when, in 1921, the Custom House went up in flames. Guinness barges were unloading on the quay outside the building when they were ordered by the military to get to hell out of the place – or else!

In 1922, during an early morning Civil War attack on the Liffey-side Four Courts, the barges were due to sail at 3.30am. To sail or not to sail? In spite of gunfire across the Liffey, and allowing for the fact that only skippers remained on deck, the fleet sailed and delivered the goods. In fact the fleet never missed a sailing during that week of intense military activity and, as a reward, the Company gave the crews an extra week's wages.

The 1930s saw a decline in the use of barges. This was partly due to the opening of a Guinness brewery in London in February 1936, which resulted in less stout going to England from Dublin and partly because of the introduction of lorries for transporting stout to Dublin port. Four barges were sold off. One went under her own power to work at Scapa Flow in Scotland (where the surrendered German fleet was scuttled in 1919); another sailed to the Humber in the northeast of England via the Caledonian Canal; yet another Guinness barge went to war at Dunkirk in 1940 and did her bit.

The 1939–45 war gave a new lease of life to the barge fleet. The remaining six barges came back into their own as the main means of transport between St James's Gate and the port. Quite often they made two trips a day – despite the low-grade fuel available as power. Indeed they often had to use timber to light up the fire plus a kind of mangled coal or slack aptly called 'duff'. And yet, in spite of all these difficulties, it is claimed that not once was there even one minute's delay in the sailing time of any of the cross-channel ships during the war which could be attributed to the barges.

After the war, transport eventually returned to normal. Diesel and petrol became available again. The cost of the barges, and especially the cost of the very considerable handling which was necessary, had to be compared with the very much lower cost of transport by road. With the advent of tanker-ships the bell began to toll for the barges. By mid-1961 the end came. They left the Liffey for various destinations. Some went to the Shannon where they were used for the movement of sand dredged from Lough Neagh. Others saw service on the canals of Ireland. One or two of them were converted into luxury homes on water! The jetty at St James's gate is no more. Not a trace. *Sic transit...*

And so ends an eighty-eight-year chapter about a part of Guinness which was an integral part of Dublin and of Ireland. And a sight which no overseas visitor to Ireland could ever forget. As luck would have it I found myself on the last barge to sail on Guinness business up the Liffey. I was recording the event for a radio broadcast and we now have on tape what is possibly the only record of the sound of a Guinness barge puffing its noisy but friendly way along under the bridges. The recording is now in the archives of RTÉ. Thus is preserved the sound of Guinness!

Coopers

The hoil, the cross, the crummy-knife, the chince, the rushing iron, the bick (or beck) iron, the swift, tit-lark, round-shave, mall. We are talking about the year 1666, the year that the Regular Dublin Coopers' Society received its Royal Charter from Charles II. They've kept it ever since. The skill and craftsmanship of coopers in the practice of their cask-caring over heaven knows how many centuries resulted in the gradual introduction of tools bearing the names listed above.

The cooper makes casks. And casks hold beer. So coopering and brewing are twinned like bacon and eggs, fish and chips, cricket and bats. Apart from their arcane language, there are many other interesting things about coopers which any story about Guinness must highlight. They have always occupied a unique place in the hierarchical structure of the Brewery. They were, so to speak, set apart from other employees partly by the nature of their working (they used the piece-time method) but also because of the long history of their craft. They were fiercely jealous of their royal charter. They worked very hard and very skilfully. They made new casks, sent them off about their business of carrying Guinness all over the place, taking them back for checking after each trip, and breaking them up after an average life-span of ten years. Whatever was left of each cask by way of re-usable wood was salvaged and became part of a new cask. So the cycle re-started.

In the late 1800s and beginning of the 1900s there were some 300 coopers at St James's Gate. Because Guinness was the largest employer of coopers in Ireland, Guinness set the rates of pay for coopers. In 1920 the basic pay for Guinness coopers was ninety-eight shillings a week, but payment for various grades of coopers ranged from 104 to 155 shillings a week.

The amount of work required of coopers often varied with sales. When sales were bad, work declined. Such was the agreement between coopers and Company that, when that happened, piece-work pay was not allowed to exceed ordinary time pay rates. Again, there was no problem in reaching agreement between Company and coopers about an increase in the number of coopers' apprentices in the Brewery.

For a very long time Brewery coopers had their own 'sick club' — a means of paying a weekly allowance to coopers on the sick list. Each cooper donated sixpence a week as a membership fee and the club had its own medical

CHARITY

Perhaps it is partly because they learned from the charitable and caring attitude of the Company, but whatever the reason, many of the people who work in Guinness have devoted a great deal of their leisure time to helping others who were less fortunate. The personal charitable work done by Guinness people is immense.

An establishment for looking after mentally handicapped children, run by the Brothers of St John of God at Celbridge (the birthplace of Arthur Guinness), for example, needed a sheltered workshop so that the children could learn to do useful work and so to take a more active part in ordinary life. Guinness personnel got involved in this project in a voluntary way and, within a very few years, they raised £3000 (about £24,000 in today's money) – enough to build the workshop.

Another Guinness group devoted its efforts to organising an annual party in Dublin for hundreds of orphans from the city and from various parts of the country. Long before the Vatican Council's suggestions about greater contact between all Christian communities, members of the Guinness Film Society brought together children and their guardians from all denominations to an annual Christmas show in

Dublin. Special buses were chartered to cater for those living at some distance from the city. Some wonderful things happened at those parties – like the time when children from different orphanages came together for the party and amongst them were found a brother and a sister who had not seen each other for years.

Other charitable undertakings included boys' clubs run outside the Brewery with many Guinness personnel on their committees; the Godparents' Society which looked after children during their formative years – with Guinness people helping to organise things; the St Brigid's Conference of the St Vincent de Paul Society, membership of which was confined to Guinness employees who were themselves confined to the Brewery for raising funds. And among employees there were leaders of Boys' Brigade groups, of Girls' Brigade groups, of Boy Scout troops and of boys' clubs.

officer. As an industrial relations gesture (it wasn't called that at the time, of course) the Company gave an annual subscription (about £200) to the club which equalled the total annual payments made by coopers.

Another indication of the somewhat unusual relationship between coopers and Company arose in November 1921 when general economic conditions in England and Ireland were bad, sales of beer suffered, and profits dropped. Companies had to take corrective action via cost reductions, including a reduction in basic wages.

When it came to dealing with the coopers, the Company was surprised to find a very strong opposition to any reduction. One of the reasons put forward by the coopers was that 'the cost of living in Dublin is higher than the cost of living in English cities'. That might well have been news to the Company! At any rate Guinness realised that, not only was it the biggest employer of coopers in Ireland, it was also a fact that the coopers had 'nobody else to look to in Ireland for employment'. Nevertheless, the proposed Company reduction in piece-time pay and piece-time work was very minimal as was its proposed reduction from seven and fourpence to seven shillings an hour, basic pay.

Entering the twentieth century, Guinness coopers were making about 34,000 new casks and breaking up about 9000 old casks per annum. At the same time they were keeping 100,000 casks in good order and condition. The more the export trade developed, the longer it took empty casks to come back home to Dublin and therefore the more casks had to be made. Around this time it was reckoned that there was a total stock of some 320,000 casks which, if these were all full, would hold 41 million pints of Guinness.

On a slack day in the cooperage, someone had the time to work out that the stock of Guinness casks at any one time was such that, laid head to head, they would stretch from London to Edinburgh or, if piled in a pyramid, would be as high as the Eiffel Tower. And all of these casks were made by Guinness coopers from the best of American white oak, though a small amount of oak also came from the Memel district in the Baltic.

Long experience had proved that oak was the only wood that had the strength and the grain required to withstand the strains and hard wear of brewery trade. At the time Irish oak, apart from being scarce, was too short in the grain and too full of knots to be of any use. Oak for the brewing trade was grown specially in large forests where the trees, in pushing up to the light, formed long lengths of straight grain with a minimum of knots and branches.

Until not so long ago there was space in all our passports for 'occupation'. I often wondered what would the passport checker at border checks think when the word 'smeller' was in that box! Yet that was one of the areas of work done by coopers. When a wooden cask came back from trade into the Brewery there was a routine for handling it. First, its branded number was recorded. Then a cooper examined it for damage. Then he removed the bung and put his nose into the hole and smelt. Depending on his trained and acute sense of smell he was able to decide what category of special cleansing was required or if the cask could join the great majority for normal washing.

As for carrying out repairs it was always a toss-up as to whether the work was more or less fascinating than making

a new cask *ab initio*. In either case there was a total absence of any modern gadgets or measuring gizmos. It was done by eye and hand – and the list of tools quoted at the opening of this section.

Alas, time marches relentlessly onwards. So it did for wooden casks and for coopers. For a whole series of reasons the use of wood for brewing vessels and for casks has almost ceased. Metal is the order of the day and not least because it can be cleaned much more thoroughly than wood and thereby achieve a much higher degree of sterility than wood – an important consideration in maintaining the quality of the beer. It also makes for a longer life of the vessels plus very reduced costs of maintenance and handling.

When the news filtered through at St James's Gate that metal was coming in and wood going out, all ranks were saddened. It wasn't just the change of materials used. It was spelling the end of an operation in the Brewery which had been there since the place was established. It was starting to say goodbye to all those generations of men who had practised their craft with such skill and dedication. No longer would the cry 'Cooper' ring out as men loading full casks would spot a leaker and scream for the coopers' equivalent of Elastoplast and the trained para-cooper to apply it effectively.

But then came a reprieve. All was not yet lost. What about all that wood stored for new casks that would now never be made? Besides, there was wood also from existing casks — what could be done with that? Enter Cinderella's fairy godmother's wand. If a pumpkin can be turned into a golden coach, why not cooper's wood into furniture?

And so was set up a new factory for turning out designs of all sorts of furniture whose elegance and craftmanship enhance households and offices and pubs and heaven-knows-what all over the world. Guinness coopers who had been transferred to non-coopering work in other parts of St James's Gate were recalled to their stalls in the Cooperage, where designs were worked out, wood was prepared, costings were estimated, price-lists were made available, marketing and sales techniques were introduced and, within a very short space of time, £20,000 worth of goods were sold. The items have found homes all over the world but especially in Ireland, the UK and the USA.

Wood which once held Guinness had become a beer tankard or a turf barrel, a whiskey keg or an ashtray, an umbrella stand or a high stool. Some of the smaller casks (kilderkins and firkins) were sawn in half, the hoops dog-nailed and painted black, the staves painted green — and voilà! A strong, handsome tub for growing shrubs or even for use on the farm as animal feeding troughs. Last but not least, some casks have ended up (of all places) in pubs, where they are used as tables or upholstered stools. The whiff of a pint sitting on the top of an ex-kilderkin can do nothing but enhance the flavour of the pint and perhaps bring a slight frisson to a stave or two of the table.

And now the furniture-making too is over. The cask wood is all used up long since. And the coopers have left. Some are on retirement. Some have passed on. So ends another chapter of the life and times of people who worked at St James's Gate. A race apart. And a craft to match. Nobody now shouting 'Cooper'. And nobody to answer the call.

The Guinness fleet

At 1700 hours on the afternoon of 12 October 1917 the SS *W.M. Barkley* slipped out of Dublin port heading for Britain. She had a full cargo and a crew of thirteen. Two hours later, one mile from the Kish lightship, she was torpedoed by a German U-boat and sank within minutes. Four of the crew, including the master and chief engineer, were lost. One of the survivors, Thomas McGlue, takes up the story:

> We rowed away from the *Barkley* in a lifeboat so as not to get dragged under and then we saw the U-boat lying astern. There were seven Germans in the conning tower all looking down at us through binoculars. We hailed the captain and asked him to pick us up. He called us alongside and asked us the name of our ship, the cargo she was carrying, who the owners were, where she was registered and where she was bound for. He spoke better English than we did. We told him the name of the ship was the SS *W.M. Barkley*, the owners were Arthur Guinness and Company, and the cargo was a load of Guinness's stout. He went below and checked

out the details we had given him. He came up and told us we could go and pointed out the shore lights to us and told us to steer for them.

Then the submarine slipped away and we were left alone with hogsheads of stout bobbing all around us. The *Barkley* had broken and gone down quietly. We tried to row for the *Kish* but it might have been America for all the way we made. We got tired and my scalded hand was hurting. We put out the sea anchor and sat there shouting all night. At last we saw a black shape coming up. She was the *Donnet Head*, a collier bound for Dublin. She took us aboard and tied the lifeboat alongside. We got into Dublin at 5am and an official put us in the Custom House where there was a big fire.

That was welcome because we were wet through and I'd spent the night in my shirt sleeves. Then a man came in and asked 'Are you aliens?' 'Yes,' said I, 'we're aliens from Dublin.' He seemed to lose interest then so we walked out and got back into the lifeboat and rowed it up to the Custom House Quay. The Guinness superintendent there produced a bottle of brandy and some dry clothes and sent one of us off to hospital to have his leg seen to. The rest of us went over to the North Star for breakfast.

And later, after I'd had my arm dressed – the doctor said the salt water had done it good – the superintendent gave me a drayman's coat to wear and put me in a cab. I was glad to get back to Baldoyle because I'd left my wife sick and I was afraid she'd hear about the torpedoing before I could get home.

So ended the saga of the end of the first of the Guinness cross-channel ships. It was the first of a line which served the Company from 1917 to 1977. They had homely names like *Carrowdore*, *Clarecastle*, *Guinness*, *Clareisland*. Then came the Guinness 'ladies' – *Lady Gwendolen*, *Lady Grania*, *Lady Patricia*. Models of the *Guinness* and of the *Lady Patricia* are now in the Guinness Museum at St James's Gate. And then, in 1976, the *Miranda Guinness* – the world's first beer-tanker vessel – also on view in the museum as a model.

These were the ships which plied their way between Dublin and (mostly) Liverpool and Manchester. During their lifetime they transported over 60% of the total production at St James's Gate to the British ports. From there it was distributed all over England, Scotland and Wales whilst a great deal of it was bottled at Liverpool and distributed from there to the four corners of the globe.

Crews of the cross-channel ships were Guinness employees with special qualifications ranging from captain to rating. They had all the rights and perks of those working in St James's Gate including pensions and health-care for themselves and their families. And they had a reputation for the ship-shape and trim condition of their ships at all times and under all conditions. They carried a crew of some fourteen, with a cabin for each man.

Navigation equipment was the best available and each also had VHF radio telephone, a Marconi ship-to-shore radio equipment and a depth recorder.

Three of these ships, *Carrowdore, Clareisland and Clarecastle* were commandeered by the Admiralty during World War I and were used to coal the British Atlantic fleet. At least one of them was also used to ferry hay for the cavalry units of the British army in France – undignified for a Guinness ship but necessary!

In World War II the *Carrowdore*'s career almost ended when it was bombed by a German plane. The incident happened in 1941 and, oddly enough, very near the spot where the SS *Barkley* went down. The plane came in over the ship, dropped its bomb, and cleared off again. The bomb came in at an angle, struck the bow-rail of the *Carrowdore*, left its fin attached to the rail, and carried on into the sea where it exploded without doing any damage. A miraculous escape! The fin of the bomb is on view to this day as a souvenir at St James's Gate.

All of the later ships in the Guinness fleet had air-conditioned holds so that an even temperature was maintained while cargo was aboard. The capacity of these ships varied from ship to ship but, in all, and for several years of their working lives, they collectively accounted for some 5 million pints of Guinness leaving Dublin port every week for destinations known and unknown.

From 1917 to 1977 was a good innings but, like most things, it had to come to an end. First there was the Guinness brewery built near London in 1936 which reduced the amount of Dublin-brewed Guinness required for the British market. Then, over the years following World War II, we saw the opening of several Guinness breweries in traditional Guinness overseas markets like Nigeria. Again that reduced the quantity of exports from Dublin.

Then came the demise of wooden casks and the introduction of metal ones. That was followed by a switch from casks to large beer tanks. And finally the introduction of road tankers from Brewery to port and the pumping of Guinness from shore to ship. Finally it became obvious that it was at least as efficient and also substantially less expensive for Guinness to use hired cross-channel transport than to maintain its own fleet. This ended sixty years of Guinness ships on the Irish Sea.

On 11 June 1963, the SS *Guinness*, built in 1931, left Dublin port on her final voyage. As she edged into the middle of the Liffey her sister ship, the *Lady Gwendolen*, which was tied up at Custom House Quay, saluted her with a series of blasts on her siren. The *Guinness* replied with a single, grateful and dignified blast. On her way down-river there was many a wave from onlookers and from crews of berthed ships. As she passed the famous Hailing Station (the Liffey observation station) for the last time there was a slight hiccup. For years the *Guinness* had passed out of the port with a shout from the master 'SS *Guinness* bound for Manchester.' This time the shout was different. 'SS *Guinness* bound for Faslane.' Silence. Then came a surprised 'What?'

Again, the master called 'SS *Guinness*, bound for Faslane, Dunbartonshire.' Again a silence. Then the reply: 'Good luck.' Faslane was the home of Shipbreaking Industries Ltd at Port Shandon, Helensburgh.

At the Baily lighthouse she passed the inward-bound MV *Lady Grania* whose crew was lined up on deck for a last sight of a dear old friend and comrade. After 'Godspeed' siren exchanges, and much sailors' badinage, the *Guinness* continued the journey to her final destination at an elegant speed of 12 knots. At 0800 hours on 12 June 1963, the SS *Guinness* berthed at the wharf of Shipbreaking Industries Ltd at Faslane. At 0810 hours the master rang the engine-room to telegraph 'FWE – Finished With Engines'. The old lady had said 'goodbye'.

The Guinness railway

The trains inside St James's Gate were one of the first things to grab the attention of young fellows coming into the place at fourteen years of age. The railway system inside the walls covered a total of several miles. When it was started, the wagons were pulled along by horses and it was not until 1875 that steam locomotives, run on coal, were introduced. Later they changed to diesel. But meantime it was a man called Samuel Geoghegan, the Guinness chief engineer from 1874 to 1901, who designed an engine precisely to suit the requirements of the Brewery. Each engine had two cylinders mounted above the boiler to keep working parts away from ground dirt. The Brewery had

twenty of these made. They were to transport raw materials to wherever they were needed in the plant; to carry full casks to the various loading bays for subsequent transfer to rail, road and waterways; and to transport empty casks from whever they re-entered the Brewery to the Cooperage Department for inspection, washing, storing etc.

But to come back to Geoghegan and his inventive mind. As horses were replaced by locos two problems arose. The first was that when the Brewery narrow-gauge (1ft, 10inch) railway system was built in 1874–8 it could deal only with the engines designed by Geoghegan, which obviously could not work on any other size of gauge. Since it was far more flexible to allow the broad-gauge wagons and engines of Coras Iompair Éireann (or the Great Southern and Western Railways as it used to be called) to come into the loading bays in the Brewery to collect the goods or off-load empties, the obvious answer was to make the entire Guinness railway system capable of dealing with both gauge sizes.

So Geoghegan designed and had built what he called a 'converter frame' or 'haulage truck' which was a kind of metal cradle which sat on its four wheels on the broad-gauge (5ft, 3inch) rails. Then, by using a hydraulic hoist, the small engine was lifted off its narrow-gauge rails and placed inside the cradle with its four wheels connected up to the four wheels of the cradle so that power was transferred from the Geoghegan engine to the Geoghegan cradle.

The second problem for Geoghegan was that the

Continued on page 91

The Front Gate of St James's Gate in the same place as it was in 1759. Over the gate is the head of Bacchus, the Roman god of wine.
Since Guinness stout is known as the 'wine of the country' it makes sense to have him over the front gate.
The date on the left remains unchanged, but the date on the right is changed on 1 January each year.

*'Digging out a kieve.' When the liquor is drained off, the floor of the kieve is left with
hot, spent grain which was shovelled into the centre outlet and down into wagons
below. It was hot work done by men wearing protective clogs and little else.
An extra pint was given to kievesmen to ward off dehydration.*

Turning the malt on the malt-house floor. Traditionally the men wore
loose-fitting flannel clothes and used large-headed, wooden shovels for the job.
To avoid damaging the malt grains they did their work in bare feet.

Storing the 1947 crop of hops. The smell of hops is said to be good for insomnia but this was never classified as an occupational hazard at St James's Gate!

The 'pulling-in' process at the windlass. It was at this stage that the object took on the appearance of a cask. Tension was brought about by the tightening of a steel hawser, which closed all joints.

Nearly there. With the staves held taut by steel hawsers the chime hoop is being hammered into position. This operation is called 'trussing the staves into shape' in the craft.

Warming the staves of the cask to make them more pliant — which made it easier to put on the binding hoops

The Guinness Cooperage c 1900. Not exactly an attractive sight,
but not uncommon in those days.

*A drayman, dressed in typical attire, drinking his well-earned pint at a
brewery tap. Having delivered thousands of pints to thirsty Dubliners all day,
the least he could expect was one for himself.*

A cooper making hoops for a cask, c 1963

A repair job.
The defective stave is removed, a new stave fitted, hoops put back in place and the repaired
cask sent off for a thorough cleaning before its next trip to heaven-knows-where.

The Cooperage Yard, c 1930. The building in the centre is the office block or departmental administration HQ. Note the number of men around the area which, years later and with the introduction of mechanical handling, led to major reductions in personnel costs.

A snowy day in the Cooperage Yard

Apart from making new wooden casks and repairing damaged ones, coopers were trained to know by smell whether or not a returned empty was 'sweet' or in need of special cleansing. A keen sense of smell and an experienced nose was the best way of finding out — smell it and see. . .

*Lord Boyd, then MD of the Guinness Group, racking the last wooden cask
ever to be used at St James's Gate. It was the end of over two centuries of using
wooden casks. Their metal successors can be seen lurking in the background
ready to go into trade.*

Wooden vats. It was part of the whole post-war reconstruction of the brewery that wood was replaced by metal. Inset you see a six-footer brewery policeman measuring up to a vat. He was the head of the brewer police and, as it happens, my Uncle Tom.

*Guinness coppers. You can read about them on the notice and you can see some
bales of hops on the landing above them ready to be off-loaded into them.
It is easy to imagine the impression made on me, a fourteen-year-old,
when I was introduced in 1938 to this wondrous brewing scene.*

Up the steps and through the front door of the St James's
Gate Brewery. Inside the front hall a liveried porter said
'Good Morning, sir!'

Continued from page 74

Brewery was built on two levels. So in order to allow the narrow-gauge transport system to operate on, and between, both layers a tunnel was built underneath the plant. It was a spiral tunnel with a total length of 864 feet and with just over two and a half turns to cope with its gradient of one in forty. It was the corkscrew method used for example at the 14.8km St Gotthard Tunnel in Switzerland.

It was always a joy to watch this Guinness railway in action. The great dream of any young lad was to get a lift through the tunnel but I never heard of any lad achieving this. We used to watch the train vanishing down the mouth of the tunnel in the Brewery yard and we could monitor its progress as it spewed up smoke and steam through the ventilation covers in the Brewery yard as it puffed its way down to the lower level. There it would suddenly emerge, huffing and puffing and hooting. Both driver and guardsman had faces covered in the grime collected on the trip. We learned that the trip in the tunnel was the only time the guardsman was able to get a lift on the engine. At all other times he had to walk in front of the train with red flag and whistle.

A similar procedure had to be adopted when the broad-gauge engine and wagons left on the 600-yard journey from the Brewery to the marshalling yards of the railway company. This rail link between Guinness and the railway dates back to 1874. It was quite a sight to behold this mammoth engine and its long line of thirty wagons making its cautious way very slowly along the public road 'twixt Brewery and railway yards at Kingsbridge (now Heuston) Station. Ahead went the man with the red flag. There was a large brass bell mounted on the engine which clanged its warning way all along the route and I often wondered why it sounded so serious when it might have played some happy little jingle. But it was yet another part of Guinness out on parade in Dublin streets and admired by all who saw it. But who could put a PR value on this necessary part of the bringing of Guinness to all parts of the country?

Came May 1965 and road transport won the financial battle for the business of transporting Guinness. Costings showed the advantages of the switch. But, as in all such matters of comparative costs, no thought seems to be given to such extremely important factors as the cost of pollution by lorry noise, by fuel vapour emissions, traffic congestion and delays, traffic accidents, wear and tear on the health of operatives and other road users etc.

Promotion!

I was now sixteen. I was earning a little extra money by way of cash prizes for passing my annual exams in the subjects I was learning at the Tech. That was very handy for buying those few extras which my weekly wages could not do. Apart from the odd brush with my boss I was, apparently, giving satisfaction.

The Vathouses

I had been a member of the No. I Thomas Street unit of messengers for over two years when, one day, I was told I was being promoted. I was to report for duty as the sole messenger attached to the Vathouses Department. That meant that I was on my own from now on and answerable directly to the manager of the Vathouses Department. Although, in theory, my only boss in my new job was the manager of the department, the practicality was that all ten or so staff members of the department were my bosses. They were all members of the laudable No. I Staff and all male. They were addressed as 'sir' by the departmental workforce and by me. They were very nice people. Several of them had served as officers in the 1914–18 war and they had long since learned how to earn and keep the respect of the people under them.

Believe it or not, I was given my own office! True, it was only marginally bigger than a match-box and the furniture consisted of one chair and a table no bigger than a draining board. But there was no denying the fact that Byrne had an office. And one of the first things I did was to put up a

THE BREWERY

The Brewery where all this brewing of Guinness has been going on since 1759 started as a derelict St James's Gate, when Arthur I took it over. At the time, there were about a hundred operating breweries in Ireland. Even small towns like Naas and Wexford each had four breweries. Birr had seven, Foxford had five. Dublin had twelve — and these twelve collectively accounted for 50% of the total amount of beer produced in Ireland. By 1920 there were only four breweries left in Dublin.

In 1759, the brewing equipment at St James's Gate consisted of the following:

3 marble chimney pieces, 1 kitchen grate rack and shelves, 2 small fixed grates, 11 troughs, 1 float, 1 kieve, 2 brass cocks, 1 underback, 1 copper, 2 underback pumps, 6 oars, 1 strike, 1 horse mill, 1 hopper, 1 pan of stones, 1 box of drawers, 1 desk, 1 office.

Also on the four-acre site were stables for twelve horses and a loft which could hold 200 tons of hay (presumably for the horses). Since the whole brewery had been out of action for at least ten years at this point, production was nil. But, at its best, this little brewery would have had a potential total annual output of about 10,000 gallons of ale.

Today, on a site which has grown to 64 acres, the most technologically advanced brewery in Europe produces half a million gallons per day. And today's brewery is so designed that it can and does produce almost all the drinks that can be called 'beer'.

A visit to St James's Gate Brewery today is quite an experience. It's not unlike a space ship with its countless computer screens, flashing lights, and very few people. On a recent visit I was shown panels of computer keys under the control of one operator. He told me that he and his fail-safe equipment between them were doing the work which used to be done by ninety-eight men. That fact may be enough to convey the extent of the change from a puny brewery in 1759 to the Brobdingnagian St James's Gate of today.

calendar on the wall — but I had to change it myself every day.

Being in the Vathouses meant that I was now, so to speak, in the production line. My job in those days was an endless series of journeys all over the production area carrying books and ledgers from one office to another. These books contained important figures about technical things such as temperatures, gravities, alcoholic content and measurements of the vast quantities of stout in those gargantuan vats and other brewing vessels. This was my introduction to the actual production of what, even then, I knew to be the most famous stout in the world and its production in the largest stout brewery in the world. It was both awesome and exciting and between the ages of sixteen and eighteen I knew I was at the hub of things.

At times I was called on to wash various little glasses which held samples. I also had to wash thermometers which had been dipped into samples of stout. And I had to keep the saccharometers clean. A saccharometer is an instrument used in brewing to measure the amount of sugar in a solution and thus gives the specific gravity of that solution. It is about nine inches long and made of glass. It looks like an elongated sausage and is calibrated. It had to be handled with great care. Even being able to pronounce its name gave me a kick. I was on the threshold of science!

In the brewing process, vats have three main functions. They are vessels for storing beer, for maturing it, and for mixing two or more beers to achieve a desired end product. The work of the Vathouses is, for several reasons, very tricky. One reason is because of the number of vats and their capacity. For instance a St James's Gate vat can hold 722,600 pints of Guinness. Multiply that by some 64 vats and you can work out the total capacity in vat at any one time. Multiply that again by the price of the pint in a pub and you will find the approximate total value of the stout in vat — and you will get some idea of the assets being managed in a vathouse. So before you start opening and closing vat inlets and outlets you had better be quite certain

what you are doing or you may inadvertently raise the level of the River Liffey and turn its water an even deeper shade of brown. The only beneficiaries of such a mistake are whatever fish swim in the Liffey, who get a bumper binge!

The system of checks and double-checks, locks and keys, staff and employees involved in the management of this whole operation more or less ensured that mistakes were not made. But nothing in life is risk-free. And things can go wrong. On the few occasions that beer found its way out of St James's Gate in a beer main rather than via more conventional and less wasteful modes of transport there was the mother and father of a post-mortem when almost everyone and every detail of procedures were under scrutiny. I thought the guilty would be shot at dawn.

One of the great problems with wooden vats was the cleaning of them. The routine was to lower a lighted candle on a string right down to the floor of the vat to be cleaned. If the candle remained lighted that meant that there was no question of unwanted brewing gases such as carbon dioxide remaining in the vat and it was safe for the men to proceed to clean it. Down went the team complete in their rubber boots, waterproof pants and jacket, waterproof hat, with brushes and water hoses. After hours of very hard work hosing and scrubbing the inside of the monster it was at last fit for use again.

It is extremely difficult to do a really thorough job of washing the insides of wooden vessels like vats or casks. You just can't clean wood completely. Indeed, in the brewing and distilling industries, it is arguable whether you really want to achieve such a high degree of sterility even if you could, since alcohol is its own steriliser; besides, spirits and beers leave behind in their vessels the clean and wholesome aroma of what they contained. Nowadays brewing vessels (and most casks) are made of metal and are thoroughly cleaned automatically like articles in a domestic dishwasher. It is all done by highly sophisticated technology and controlled by computer. Desirable left-over aromas are a thing of the past and old-time pint drinkers will claim, wistfully, that they have been sterilised out of existence – the beer vessels, that is, not the drinkers!

Anyway here was I in 1940, the smallest cog in an exciting wheel of frenetic activity, playing my walk-on part with, I hope, due gravity. When I eventually left the Vathouses Department in 1942 I was very sorry to go. I felt I had been working in the very heart of this old Brewery and the lovely aroma of the place had penetrated into my very being. I got to know every nook and cranny of the old Vathouses and I had begun to look on the place with an almost proprietorial attitude. And I got to know Joe Naughton.

Joe Naughton

As with any production company there is a special nomenclature used to describe various components of the production processes and jobs held by the people involved in these processes. One job in the Vathouses had the title of 'charger'. I suppose the word comes from being a 'charge hand' or being 'in charge of' something. Anyway there were some five or six chargers in the Vathouses. Joe Naughton was one of them. Chargers were distinguishable by a kind of brown cotton coat they wore. They were the link between the 'staff' (officers) and the men (troops) – a kind of senior NCO.

Joe had served in the 1914–18 war as a stretcher-bearer on the battle field. His job was to go out amid the chaos and mud and bring in the wounded and the dead. He helped to bury the dead and to hand over the wounded to the medics for treatment. It surely had a very strong effect on a man. In the course of duty he met a Scottish nurse called Janet. They eventually married and produced two children. One was a most attractive daughter who became a nurse in World War II, met a dashing young pilot officer in the Australian air force, married him and went to Australia where she has lived ever since. Her only sibling was a boy called Douglas James. More of him in a moment.

Looking back now I realise that, like my brothers, I was born and brought up with a large streak of what might be called divine discontent. I'm rarely if ever satisfied with my performance or my lot. From my mother we had inherited a very strong gene of ambition. She constantly reminded us that we had two options about how we would get on in life. We could either settle for the kind of life she and my father lived or we could 'go for it' and do a great deal better. It was all up to us. And any obstacles to our future achievements were entirely imaginary. Just remove them and get on with things. And the rewards would be great. But we were not to settle for the humdrum or we'd spend our lives frustratingly regretting it.

To me, Joe Naughton was an example of someone who had settled for the humdrum and spent his life regretting it. He had had an ordinary education up to the age of fourteen but no academic life after that. But he was highly intelligent and he felt that he had in some way squandered his life and that it was now too late to do anything about it. He was just a charger in the vathouses of a brewery in Dublin and would remain there until pensioned off at the age of sixty-five. He saw no good reason why he should not have been the managing director of the Brewery. He had simply not made enough use of his talents.

But Joe was nothing if not pragmatic. So he switched his frustrations about his own career and life and used the otherwise idling energy to see to it that the same would not happen to his children. His daughter was well educated up to the age of eighteen and then she went on, like her mother, to be trained in one of life's most worthy professions – that of nurse.

The boy Douglas had a first-class schooling in Dublin and then, to the delight and pride of his parents, entered one of the world's best medical schools, at Trinity College, Dublin. His schooling, and subsequent six-year course in Trinity meant a very considerable cost which could not be met by a weekly Guinness wage packet. So both parents

earned it by extra-mural work of various kinds over a long period. It was a very hard slog – but it was a labour of love. Douglas lived up to their sacrifices. He was a very handsome chap. He had a brilliant medical school record, became captain of Trinity Boat Club, qualified with an excellent degree and took up his first job as a general practitioner in a small village called Ballytore in County Kildare. He was everything Joe himself would want to have been but wasn't.

Like many another Trinity student or recent graduate in 1942, Douglas decided that he should do his bit in the war and so he joined the Royal Navy as a surgeon lieutenant. His first posting was as ship's surgeon on the cruiser HMS *Curaçao*. On his first time at sea, the giant liner *Queen Mary* collided with *Curaçao*, splitting it in two, and hundreds of men were drowned, including Douglas.

The Naughtons never recovered from this awful tragedy. Stoically they decided on an anodyne – work. They set to and started breeding pedigree dogs. Janet did some private nursing. Anything to keep them busy and to help assuage the hurt and feeling of desolation and total loss.

It was during this period that I entered their lives. To say that I became a surrogate son would be a gross and unfair exaggeration. I was almost eighteen. No money. And no hope whatever of any worthwhile advance in Guinness because of the way the personnel maze was structured. In fact, the best I could hope for was the possibility of a job as a Vathouse charger like Joe.

So, to use a bridge term, I was vulnerable. So were the Naughtons. Maybe that's how and why the relationship started and developed. Maybe I was a sort of project they took on. They knew that I was studying at tech in the evenings but that wasn't really leading to any kind of worthwhile qualification. They also knew that I had to earn a living because my parents needed the money to help raise younger siblings. That meant I couldn't attend daytime education of any kind. But they had also decided that, like Douglas, I should go to Trinity — come what might! Unlike me at that time, they were not to be put off by the fact that, as a Roman Catholic, I was not allowed to attend Trinity without the express permission of the Archbishop of Dublin.

To try to deal with this tangle of problems they frequently invited me out to visit them in their home at Killester. (Joe referred to it as Killester-on-sea!) This was one of a cluster of cottages offered to soldiers returning home after World War I. (They were said to be 'homes fit for heroes'. Joe's sense of humour led him to the view that 'You'd have to be a hero to live in them!') The house of the Naughtons was full of books of all kinds and that was for me the start of a lifetime of well-nigh voracious reading.

How this whole matter of my future career turned out will be unfolded shortly. The main point I'm making here is that, as a result of my perfectly ordinary transfer from No. 1 Thomas Street to the Vathouses Department, I met someone which resulted in my life never being the same

again. Nothing new about such happenings. But, in my forty-year odyssey through the labyrinth of the Guinnesss organisation, my two-year sojourn in the Vathouses, which led to my meeting Joe Naughton must stand as a milestone.

Number-taking

Late in 1942 I was instructed to sit for what was called the 'Number-takers Examination'. 'Number-takers' had started life at St James's Gate as boys, but once you reached eighteen, you became what was officially classified as a 'lad'. Some lads did labouring work of one kind or another; most became what was known as 'number-takers'. Every cask in the Brewery had a (usually) six-digit number branded on to its head by the cooper who made it. It carried that number like a fingerprint for its entire working life. Every time it left the Brewery as a 'full' a note of that movement was made. Every time it came back into the Brewery as an empty a note of its safe return was made. And the people who recorded these events were lads who worked as number-takers.

In all, there were about forty-five number-takers in the Company and the system of which they were a part ensured that, at any time, the Company knew of the whereabouts of every cask — and that meant about half a million casks. This close monitoring system meant that it was very difficult to steal a cask, or inadvertently leave it in some outhouse of a country pub, or use it for purposes for which it was never intended, because its non-return as an empty from the person to whom it was last invoiced would show up on the books and then be investigated.

This system was in operation for very many years. Then one day some genius came up with the idea that the cost of keeping cask movements policed to such a high degree was extremely expensive. He worked out that the Company could easily afford to lose quite a number of casks every year and still compensate for the cost of keeping a permanent eye on them. He was right. The system was eventually done away with and with it went forty-five number-takers' jobs plus heaven knows how many jobs of those who transferred the numbers into ledgers.

Anyway, to qualify as a number-taker, lads had to sit an exam. The idea was essentially to test your accuracy in reading the branded number on casks and your legibility in writing them down on paper – hardly a taxing task for a lively intellect. Like most lads who took this test, I passed, and I was then transferred from the Vathouses Department to the Traffic Department, which was responsible for the effective and efficient organisation and transportation of all full casks leaving the Brewery for any destination.

Working as a number-taker was a kind of three-year interlude between being a 'boy' and becoming a fully-fledged 'labourer' on the day you reached twenty-one. (For some reason which I've never been able to find out 'labourers' were also called 'tariff' men, in other words, they were considered ungraded.) In brief, number-takers worked a five-and-a-half-day, 44-hour week, but, since casks were

leaving and entering the Brewery at all hours of the day and night and all of their branded numbers had to be recorded, number-takers had to do shift work, which could see you starting and finishing anytime between 4.30am and eight or nine o'clock in the evening.

We were paid at the rate of £180 *per annum* (about £4000 in today's money). We got two weeks' paid leave *per annum* plus every Sunday and Bank Holiday off. Our weekly wage was usually, but not always, augmented by what was called 'beefer money'. This was a scheme whereby, in an attempt to ensure that the branded numbers were accurately recorded, the Company fell back on one of the oldest and best Protestant ethics of 'reward for endeavour'. In this instance it meant that number-takers were rewarded with a little something extra if they could demonstrate a high degree of accuracy. The scheme was that every number-taker was allowed a certain number of mistakes in recording which, if you did not exceed, entitled you to a monthly reward of ten shillings. This was known as 'beefer money', from an old Dublin slang word 'beefer', meaning mistake.

Some months you won your 'beefer money' – some you didn't. If you consistently failed to win it then you were severely reprimanded or even moved to less mentally taxing work. If you consistently got the award – you smiled at the unlucky with a superior, smug smile. The extra money was a godsend and the excitement on the day of each month when payouts were made put the Queen's efforts on Maundy Thursday into the shade.

A heavily subsidised lunch was available if we wanted it, but we were not provided with any free protective clothes or footwear because we rarely, if ever, worked in the open. It was certainly not a very taxing job. In fact it was what was called in Dublin slang 'a bobby's job', meaning a job that you were very lucky to have because it required no sweat or unpleasant tasks, but was a 'stroll-around' occupation such as a policeman (or 'bobby') has on the beat. Anyway we swanned along day by day doing what we were supposed to do and trying not to think of our fate when we reached manhood. That allowed us a little time to read, chat – and toughen up.

By that I mean that several of us who were interested in sports and in keeping fit voluntarily helped to load full casks on to the Guinness lorries and do it in such a way that any stevedore would approve. Of course we were not supposed to do this but, on early morning shifts during the winter months, we relished work that kept us warm and helped our fitness. Not only that but we were also learning to drive. The lorries in use at that time were huge, five-ton Latils, which had a solid iron 'gate' gear-box and handle and you had to be very strong to drive them. But in return for loading their lorries for them, and thus having them ready to set off on their journeys, a few of the lorry drivers let us sit up with them in the cab and we learned how to drive. Of course it was totally wrong of the drivers and number-takers to be involved in driving lessons and, if we had been discovered, all hell would have broken out. But while management stayed busy in their offices and foremen were writing up their books, we learned to drive.

Number-takers were a great bunch. We were all about the same age and we were interested in more or less the same things. We played soccer, snooker, tennis, cricket. We went to the pictures quite a lot. Some of us had 'mots' – an old Dublin word for a girlfriend. Some smoked. Some drank the odd bottle of Guinness. Some went to dances to see if we could pick up a mot. A few did the 'pools' every week to try and make a fortune so they could either buy or leave the Brewery.

We had a number-takers' soccer team called the 'Hurricanes'. That was the name of the Royal Air Force fighter aircraft which helped win the Battle of Britain. We went so far as to play 'away' matches in foreign fields like Belfast. While waiting for the men to set out the batches or loads of casks prior to loading them on to goods wagons (which allowed us to record their branded numbers) we sang songs and fool-acted and did all the usual things that lads of our age did.

Almost all of us were still attending the tech in the evenings but without giving much thought as to why we were doing it other than that it looked like a good idea and might come in handy sometime, somewhere. But all the time we had this faraway cloud of fatalism hanging over us, because we knew that once our three years were up and we became 'men' we were doomed to become common labourers and to remain so for the rest of our working lives.

Good, steady, secure, pensionable jobs with acceptable pay and conditions. Not bad reasoning at a time when the greatest war that ever happened on planet Earth was going on almost in our own backyard and it looked, at that time, as if the Nazi regime would triumph and Europe, including us, might well be enslaved.

A day on a barge

My father was a skipper on a Guinness barge. He had survived the 1914–18 trenches, and he was very happy with his peaceful life on the Liffey. Many's the time the Byrne children all sat at home while he told us stories about what happened on the Liffey or at the port of Dublin (he always called it the North Wall) that day. We learned and loved all about that part of the Guinness operation because it had a slight dash of danger and adventure about it all. And being able to drive one of those barges up and down the Liffey in all weathers and under a variety of conditions must (we felt) be a great and almost heroic thing to be doing every day. And doing it in the dead o'night (3.30am) made it even more mysterious and wonderful.

It was one of the dreams of young lads in Guinness to be able to travel down the Liffey on a Guinness barge. Alas, for many reasons, it was absolutely out of the question. But impossibilities are often a challenge. And so it proved. Let me explain.

The system of transporting full casks from St James's Gate to ships at Dublin port started by rolling the casks on to bogies. These little bogies were then taken by a miniature railway system on their narrow-gauge out of the Brewery and across the road outside to the jetty at Victoria Quay. There they were winched off the bogie and lowered and stowed in the hold of the barge. When the barge reached the port it lay alongside the cross-channel ships and the casks were winched out of the hold and stowed in the hold of the ship. Alternatively, the casks were sometimes off-loaded from barge to quayside and later winched into the ship's hold.

One bright morning in the summer of 1943 my butty, Bill, and myself found ourselves on a 5am shift, recording the branded numbers of casks as they were loaded on bogies prior to their departure to the port. Then tragedy struck! Whether we both dozed off or what I'm never sure (or willing to discuss), but at all events we failed to record an entire barge load of hogsheads. And before we discovered this catastrophe the barge was fully loaded and ready to slip its moorings and sail down river. There was only one thing for it. We'd have to travel down with the barge (either as stowaways or with the skipper's permission) and record the cask numbers as they swung from barge to ship.

As it happened, the barge was skippered by my father. With a wink from him we were aboard. And off we went on a journey which very few Dubliners have ever made and which any Dublin lad would have given his all to do. One by one under the bridges we went and there the thrill was twofold. It was seeing underneath bridges over which countless people walk every day without ever seeing what was under them. And the fact that, in order for the barge to fit under the bridge, the funnel of the barge was flicked down, steam and smoke was everywhere, the noise of the engine reverberated all over the place – and it was dark. True, it lasted for just a few seconds under each bridge before we came out the other side, but what a thrill!

Eventually we tied up alongside the Guinness ship and the transfer of casks from barge to ship got under way. We recorded the cask numbers, and all was saved. But just how saved it was we hadn't anticipated, because when the cargo was all safely out of the barge we moved a few yards and tied up along the quayside. Then we went below into the galley of the barge where we had the mother and father of a breakfast with the crew – eggs, bacon, fried bread, scalding tea. It was sheer bliss and something I'll never forget. I can smell it to this day!

The journey back up-river was just as enjoyable. The city was wakening up by then and every bridge had its quorum of onlookers. We waved to them and they waved to us. It was a lovely summer's morning and we were all in good form. We were all friends. We saw quay-side buildings from an angle not given to the rest of humanity. Like Gandon's majestic Four Courts with its great copper dome and his Custom House; the Wellington Monument in the Phoenix Park; Christchurch Cathedral. Eventually we tied up at the Guinness jetty and disembarked. We had done

something that morning which we'd remember for ever. Boy were we glad we'd missed those numbers!

Considering my options

It was shortly after starting number-taking that the penny dropped with me. I slowly began to realise that I had to take a decision about my future. And I had to take it now. What were my options? Well, there were at least three.

First of all I could do as most of the others would do – stay put in the Brewery. I could await my reaching the age of twenty-one and accept whatever job I was given. It could be that of lorry driver, cask roller, cask cleaner, barge rating, vat cleaner or man messenger. I might eventually even reach the dizzy heights of foreman. I'd be safe and well under the Guinness distress-proof umbrella and I would be looked after and minded until honourable pension at sixty-five and even beyond. I'd be secure.

But even then it crossed my mind that settling for security would mean that that was all I would have. And since there was absolutely no hope whatever of breaking into the commissioned ranks there was no hope of real advancement. I decided I was not going to settle for this scenario, but I had no idea how to break out of it. Still, it was obvious that to get up I'd have to get out.

Which led me to my second option, which was to stay put as I was but meantime get myself qualified as soon as possible to get a good job outside the Brewery. How would I do that? After a good deal more thought I decided that I wanted to do science because that would qualify me to get a job as a research chemist in some place such as Lever Brothers in Port Sunlight outside Liverpool. That would mean emigration but I could come home every weekend on the Liverpool–Dublin ferry so that would be fine. I'd be earning enough to continue to support the family. And I'd be near home.

Of course there was a snag. How would I get a science degree? I had long since decided, and the Naughtons confirmed this, that if ever I had the good fortune to go to a university it was Trinity or nothing. But that meant attending Trinity as a full-time student, which I could not do because I had to keep my Guinness job. Impasse.

And out of the gloom came a shaft of very pale light. Would it not be a good thing to get myself qualified to enter Trinity in the Micawber-like hope that something would eventually turn up? (Trinity Entrance was generally accepted as an examination which was easier to pass than Leaving Certificate. Whether that is so or not, it is relevant to note the policy of the College in this matter. They held the view that selection or rejection of students would take place 'not at matriculation but at later examinations when the educational machine would have had the opportunity of raising all but the unteachable to a reasonable standard, if not of culture and scholarship, then at least of literacy and information'.) Good thinking. Good decision. I set to and did some more intensive study, sat for Trinity Entrance and got it.

That did two things. It qualified me to enter one of the oldest and one of the best universities in the world, and it reaffirmed my absolute determination to do so. My mother was delighted. So were the Naughtons. So? It couldn't be done – could it? I failed to see how.

Joining up – or trying to!

That forced me into my third option. Join up and go to war. After all, my family tradition was strong in this area. My father plus seven of his siblings fought in the 1914–18 war. They were in several regiments and fought all over the place. They all came back home in one piece although one of them died shortly afterwards from the delayed effects of poison gas.

Was it my turn to go? My older brother Ray, who was working in the Chemists' Laboratory in Guinness, had joined the Irish army. Later he was to join the Royal Air Force. The Company was offering half pay to the family of anyone who volunteered for the Irish or British armed forces for as long as they were away plus a guarantee of their own job when they returned. Furthermore, quite a number of Guinness people of all ranks had joined up and many were coming back on leave with great stories of wine, women and song – and some very exciting stories of active service as well! So, what about it?

My best friend Frank was a number-taker. We lived very near each other and were life-long butties. Both our fathers worked in Guinness. We talked long and hard about joining up. Finally we decided we'd had enough of number-taking and Guinness and the gloomy future of a nothing job staring us in the face. Why not make a break and go? So without telling anyone else we took a day's leave and went up to Belfast on the train. We went to the Royal Air Force recruiting office and declared our desire to train as RAF pilots. We were quite clear what we wanted and, for a change, we had no intention of accepting anything else. We did a fairly thorough medical test and passed A1 – which meant we were physically fit to apply for any job. Then we did an education test. We passed that. Then we did an interview, declared our choice of pilot, and were accepted as trainee pilots.

For obvious reasons, and ones we did not like to dwell upon, they were running short of pilots at that stage. We were in. The score was to go back home to Dublin, get our family and employment things settled and wait about a week for the arrival of our call-up papers which would come by post. Once that happened we were to report without delay to RAF HQ in Northern Ireland. Done!

Back home and we had to tell our parents. All hell broke loose. All four parents held meetings and we were hammered, cajoled, bribed, threatened, screamed at. To show the lengths to which *my* parents went they even offered to send me to Trinity as a full-time student and were quite prepared to beg or borrow or even steal the money to do it! Of course I couldn't accept that offer either then or ever. But the fact that they made it shocked me deeply and made me realise just how completely overwrought they were at the thought of my joining up.

A week later Frank's call-up papers arrived. Mine didn't. We made a pact that one wouldn't go without the other. Family matters grew intolerable. Still my papers hadn't arrived. We stayed number-taking. Weeks went by. Somehow or other the pot went off the boil. Our enthusiasm waned. Then it sneaked away like last winter's snow. We abandoned our heroic attempt. We succumbed to the inert security of Guinness. Later, when Frank reached twenty-one, he was offered a job as a labourer. He left and joined the Royal Navy. After his two years' service he came back and was re-offered his previous job. He resigned and secured an administrative job elsewhere.

And me? It was a long time afterwards that I learned that my papers had come and my mother had put them in the fire. Meantime I still had two of my three options left. And it was while I was struggling with these problems that a second penny dropped.

Getting Around the System

I asked myself why it was that the likes of me on the shop floor – irrespective of religion – could not be considered for a job on the No. 2 Staff or, for that matter, on the No. 1 Staff. Regarding the No. 2 Staff the answer was fairly easy – I could in fact have had access to it, had it not been for an unfortunate blip in the system.

No. 2 Staff

When a 'lad' like me reached twenty-one, he was entitled to sit for the annual internal examination for entrance to the No. 2 Staff. Normally about 25 to 30 'lads' sat the exam and normally there were five or maybe six vacancies. Those who got a place were exalted to 'staff'. Those who failed to get a place went straight to the 'labourers' list. That had been the system up to 1941, but it was put on hold during the war years and my 'year' missed the opportunity. In my year all 'lads' went straight to 'labourers'. And there was no question of complaint or possibility of enquiring why this was so. It was simply the rule.

No. 1 Staff

Furthermore, there was no formal, regulated method of promotion from the No. 2 Staff to the No. 1 Staff. True, such promotions took place but they were few and far between. It happened for instance when a post such as manager was held by a No. 1 Staff person which became vacant due to the retirement or death of the holder. If the

LIFE INSURANCE

If 'employees' got perks like free beer and excursion money, members of 'staff' had other perks, for example a generous insurance scheme aimed at making provision for the dependants on the death of a staff member. In ways it was analogous to a widow's pension scheme on a contributory basis — only more valuable. It was called 'life insurance' and the scheme was established at the end of the nineteenth century.

From a selected list of first-class and approved insurance companies the staff member selected one and signed up. The member could insure to the extent of six times his or her salary to a limit of £5000. Half of this premium was paid by the staff member via monthly deductions from salary. The other half was paid, as a gift, by the Company. The policies were whole life with profits. They were held by the Company and paid only to the executors on the death of the insured.

technically to do the job was a member of the No. 2 Staff, then he might be promoted to the job and thereby move on to the No. 1 Staff. So, yes. Some transfers from No. 2 Staff to No. 1 Staff took place, but very few. And as for promotion to the No. 1 Staff from the shop floor, that was virtually unheard of. True, there were a few exceptions, like the two laboratory attendants who studied for a science degree via a London University correspondence course supplemented with laboratory work in one of Dublin's 'techs'. When they got their degrees, they were promoted to the No. 1 Staff as fully fledged research chemists, alongside other chemists who had come into Guinness as graduates. But these exceptions were very few.

But the vast majority of those appointed to the No. 1 Staff got there via a well-established procedure which had been in operation for decades. On paper it was both simple and sensible. The various steps in the procedure were almost always standard and adhered to, but the sequence of events differed now and again.

First of all there was the matter of gender. Only males were eligible, as was usual at the time for most senior jobs in Ireland and all over the world. Next came age. The range was usually eighteen to twenty-two. That left room for school-leavers, those already in jobs, university graduates, and others, and there was also some elasticity in that upper limit.

The application to the Company was in writing and would nowadays be called your CV. You included with it

obvious choice for the job happened to be a No. 2 Staff person, then he might be promoted to manager, and that was his route to the No. 1 Staff. Likewise, when a decision was taken at Board level to create a new No. 1 Staff post in some speciality area, and the person most qualified one or two letters from people who recommended you for the job. Sometimes these letters were from senior management people inside the Brewery. Sometimes from outsiders.

Then there was an interview. This meant that each candidate whose written application was deemed to suggest suitability was interviewed by the Board of Directors. Nobody quite knew the exact criteria used by the directors in determining suitability but there was, and is, nothing unusual in interviewing people for senior jobs. That said, the Board interview for appointment to the No. I Staff has always provoked wry smiles and cynical comment both from beneficiaries and others. In spite of the Guinnesses' support for Catholic emancipation, appointments made suggested that the whole procecure smacked of both religious discrimination in favour of non-Catholics and of nepotism – ironic considering that the word 'nepotism' was originally used to mean the preferment of illegitimate sons (masquerading as nephews) of popes!

The interview was crucial. If a candidate was deemed particularly suitable for appointment then marks awarded at interview could make the difference between success and failure – whichever the Board decided. But to calm down the murmurings of 'jobbery' and to be fair about it, we might consider in a moment some relevant facts about this particular aspect of the selection process.

Next came the Company-organised competitive examination, though sometimes the exam preceded the interview. Subjects included some ordinary school subjects but also there were additional subjects such as book-keeping and general knowledge. One of the Dublin commercial colleges ran a tutorial course in the exam curriculum subjects. It was an 'optional' course lasting some months and most of the candidates attended. Some 25 candidates sat the exam and competition was stiff. Depending on the number of vacancies in the Company at the time of the exam, the highest scorers were declared successful. Usually this amounted to anything from three to eight. Unsuccessful candidates could re-apply to sit the exam in the following year.

Lastly, candidates had to undergo a medical examination at the Company's Medical Centre.

The results of this whole procedure were posted out to candidates. If you were successful you were instructed where to attend at what time and on what date to start your career in the Company. You were in. As one chum said when he was told that he had made it, 'I recognised the warmth and womb-like quality of the brewery, crept in, and quickly adopted the foetal position.' Otherwise, bad luck. Perhaps try again?

Nepotism and religion

To come back for a moment to the interview aspect of this selection process and its genesis. The Guinness company was always well known for its ability to select the right people. By 'right' is meant the sort of people who were

Continued on page 115

The crew of a Guinness barge c 1950 – the skipper, the mate and three boatmen. The skipper is the one in the middle of the picture, capless and with the hand on the wheel. And he's my dad.

Guinness barges returning 'empties' to the brewery

The loading of fulls on to a canal barge at the St James's Gate harbour

Unloading of fulls at a Guinness store

*A busy, bustling day at Dublin port with the stately and stabilising influence of
the majestic Custom House in the background*

*Barges taking it easy at their berths at Victoria Quay. The buildings in the
background are part of the Traffic Department at St James's Gate.*

The Guinness barge Killiney *lying alongside* The Lady Gwendolen *at the Custom House*

*Everything in its right place and in time to catch
the tide. The skill of the stevedore was needed to
ensure correct loading and unloading.*

*Loading up the fulls by hand on to the lorries. It was
warming and muscle-building work. Number-takers often
did it as a means of warming up on a cold morning.*

A very sad scene — 12 September 1961, when the Killiney was taken from its berth at the Guinness jetty at Victoria Quay and towed away to other waters, was the last date on which there was a Guinness barge on the Liffey. It was a farewell to 88 years of Guinness barges on Anna Livia.

Guinness barges 'cruising down the river'. Because of the tides, it was sometimes a tight squeeze to arrive at each bridge with enough clearance time to get under and out again safely.

The Castleknock *carrying empties from port to jetty, July 1959*

Continued from page 106

going to make a worthwhile contribution to the Company's prosperity and success. It wasn't only family members who made it one of the world's most successful enterprises. Looking back, we can see the crucial influence and powerful contribution of people like Samuel and Thomas Grace Geoghegan, the Moravians John and John Tertius Purser, and the Huguenot Christopher Digges La Touche. These and other such men were outstanding management people, carefully selected by the family, and brought in from outside to manage the place. And the Company's extraordinary success stands as a measure of their capabilities and of good judgement in selecting them.

Secondly, there was always a touch of 'clubland' about senior Guinness management people. It was probably based on the proposition that clubs are there to keep people out rather than to let them in. Silly? Well is it? If you are running a club, or are a member of it, one of the things you don't want to happen is unsuitable people to become members of it. Because, if that happens, it discounts one of the most important attributes of a club – comfort in exclusivity. That's partly why there is a membership selection committee in clubs and also what you pay your club fee for.

There was a definite and almost palpable aura of exclusivity about the No. I Staff. So although there were no stated rules about religion or about contacts, the reality was that both counted. And the interview was where they started to count. It helped to separate the 'suitable' from the 'unsuitable'.

Thirdly we look at education and how that came into the selection process. For historical reasons, most of the important schools in Ireland were Protestant at that time, Trinity College, Dublin, the oldest university in Ireland, was Protestant and, it was believed, anti-national.

In addition to all this, there was historical distrust between the native Catholic population and the Protestant establishment, so when it came to a big employer, who was almost always a Protestant, recruiting senior staff, he was extremely careful about employing Catholics. Not only were members of the Protestant population likely to have had a better education than most Catholics, but there was also a tendency among Protestant employers to prefer to recruit from within their own population. And that is what happened in Guinness as elsewhere for two centuries. It was not until 1975 that a Roman Catholic was appointed as an executive director at St James's Gate. The justification for the system was that it worked very well and the Company thrived and prospered.

So where did all that leave a 'lad' heading for 'labourer', with only a few months of secondary education, a Roman Catholic, and with a Roman Catholic father who was on the 'labouring' list? The answer was – it left him where he was. Stuck!

Much as the system was all against me and my likes I tried not to dwell on it. I realised that, at quite a different level, I was a beneficiary of a kind of nepotism when my form of application for a job as messenger had been

'PROTESTANT PORTER'

In 1813 there was a claim that 'proposed concessions to the religious persuasions of the majority of Irish people' were opposed by a Protestant petition – and that this opposition was supported by 'the Protestant brewer Guinness'. The claim was false, but one result of this claim was a 'Protestant porter' boycott campaign when it was alleged that 'analysis of Guinness porter has shown that Brewers of anti-popery porter had mashed up Protestant bibles and Methodist hymn-books in the brew, thus impregnating in the fermentation the volatile parts of the porter with the pure ethereal essence of heresy'. The analyst went on to say that, happily, a rival brewer called Pim was producing an ale which was an antidote to the heresy porter! Presumbably Pim was a Catholic!

stamped 'Son of Employee'. Which almost certainly meant that there were boys at least as well qualified as I was to fill a vacancy but they didn't have those magic words on their forms and therefore failed to get in. You can't have it both ways!

Meantime the writing was on the wall for me. I could not get into this No. I Staff club and I was wasting my time and energy feeling cheated and angry about it. Which led me back to the necessity of staying on while I got qualified to get something worthwhile outside and then leave. So I set off on the task of getting into Trinity to do a degree.

Getting into Trinity

To do an honours degree in Trinity you had to complete each academic year by satisfactory attendance at lectures for all three terms and by passing an exam at the end of each year. There was no alternative to this. Because of my full-time job with Guinness I was unable to fulfil these requirements.

To do a pass course in Trinity you had two options. You could complete each academic year by attending lectures for all three terms and by passing an exam at the end of the academic year. Again, I could not do this. But there was also another option: by a very old rule which was rarely invoked you could also complete each academic year by attending no lectures but by passing an exam in each subject at the end of each *term*. Among other things, that meant a change every term in the course books in things like Latin, French and English plus a progression of changes in the other subjects. It also meant the loss of vital input by lectures and the loss of contact with your tutor. Not to mention the loss of that core ingredient of any true university education – just being there.

Still, I went for it. I had to. Because I had a job, I was

able to save and pay my colllege fees – helped, I want to say, by my mother's savings in running the Byrne menage. I had made an unsuccessful application to the Company for an education grant on the lines of the fees they were paying the techs for our education. The reason given for the refusal in my case was that there was no precedent for paying university fees for employees.

I found a private tutor to replace lecturers and who was willing to take me on as a student. His name was James Quinn but, for reasons I can't remember, the Byrnes always referred to him as Mickey Finn. He was a graduate of Queen's University, Belfast, and a polymath. He lived alone in garret-like quarters over a shop in Middle Abbey Street. His fees were minimal – but again I did not qualify for a Company education grant because 'there was no precedent'.

On the Staff

My row with the church

It was September 1943. I was nineteen yeas old. I was about to start on a university course next month. It was going to be a hard slog for four years. I was going to have to punch in eight hours a day plus four hours on Saturdays at Guinness and about six hours a day at study. But I wanted to do it badly enough to make me do it. All I had to do now was get permission from the Roman Catholic Archbishop of Dublin to attend the Protestant University of Dublin (Trinity College). I wrote an application for permission and that went via our parish priest to the archbishop. The PP got the reply and came and told my mother and me. It was a no.

I saw red. I saw my hopes of a decent career in ruins. I told him I was going without permission. My mother nearly died. The PP said that going to Trinity without permission would result in ex-communication, and I said I really didn't care. Details of the ensuing row are too tedious to mention. Suffice it to say that he went off in high dudgeon. Days later, he came and announced that permission was now granted – on condition that I did not join any College society or club. Brat-like, I said I would disregard that proviso. He gave up and left. The whole thing died a whimpering death.

Student/worker

During my four years at college, 1944–8, I was a number-taker in the Traffic Department of Guinness. At the time the assistant manager and later manager of the department was a man called Charles Mortier. He had come into Guinness as an expert on transport matters – a somewhat unusual method of joining the Company in those days. He was to play a crucial role in what happened to me.

In order to fulfil my requirements in my Junior Freshman (first) year, I had to sit and pass three exams between October and the following June. There was no question of either an educational grant or time off from Guinness. I had applied for both but was turned down. I was disappointed about this but I understood the rules. It was pointed out to me that, if I were given time off to attend lectures at Trinity, then how could the Company refuse someone else who sought time off to attend lessons in tin-whistle blowing? The sheer logic of that defied further questioning.

One morning in September 1944, I was on an early shift in the Brewery and finished at 3pm. I went off on my bike down Dame Street, dismounted at Trinity Front Gate and walked across Front Square with the bike to the bursar's office at the side of the Examination Hall. There I handed over an envelope with thirteen guineas inside it – in cash. That was the half-yearly fee. It was a fortune.

This money had been accumulating in a tin box under my parents' bed for months. It was made possible partly by an increase in my wages contribution to the household and also by my mother's husbandry. This was very difficult for her with a household of seven, two of whom were at school and hoping for a secondary education. Woe betide me if I wasted that fee!

Most Trinity students entered as 'pensioners'. The word originally meant one who paid a fixed sum annually. Pensioners ranked above sizars – a class of students who were allowed free education in consideration of performing certain, and at one time menial, duties. At the same time, pensioners ranked below 'fellow commoners' who paid double fees and enjoyed several privileges – like dining with the right people. Fellow commoners could finish the college degree course in three years instead of the standard four years. Briefly then it may be taken that sizars were sons of poor parents – frequently of the clergy; pensioners were sons of persons of moderate incomes; fellow commoners were sons of the wealthy or, as often happened then, of those who wished that their sons should get through college with as little delay as possible. Edward Cecil Guinness, first Lord Iveagh, for example, who graduated from TCD in 1870 with a BA degree and an MA in 1872 (and was appointed chancellor on 18 November 1908) entered Trinity in the class fellow commoners. He could certainly afford to pay for doing things in a hurry.

I saved one week of my annual holidays and, during my first term in college, I used that time to attend lectures. For me it was magic. Everything about Trinity was wonderful. I didn't fully realise at the time what was happening to me, but the place exuded learning and age and it had a style about it that, even now, is difficult to describe but palpable in the experiencing of it. It was a long time before I was mature enough to understand that the buildings themselves, the lawns, the trees, and even the very cobblestones formed a totality whose harmony results in the creation of a mood and feeling of tranquillity and ease.

I explored the buildings – including the Protestant chapel. I joined the Hist (the College Historical Society founded in 1770). I joined the Rugby Club and the Squash Club. I was bad at rugby but OK at squash. I had the odd lunch in the Dining Hall. I bought and wore a second-hand undergraduate gown – obligatory when attending lectures. I met a girl and subsequently fell in love with her. I passed my three exams and that meant I had got what was called 'credit' for my year as a Junior Freshman and was entitled and ready to become a Senior Freshman. That word 'senior' was a great boost to my morale.

Breakthrough

Then came a major breakthrough at Guinness. I had to keep in touch with my boss Charles Mortier about how things were going in college. He was, as always, most interested in how I was getting on. I reported to him about my satisfactory completion of year one and my imminent progression to year two. He was most encouraging in his reaction and reminded me to keep in touch with him. Meantime I continued as a number-taker on shift work. I also continued my visits to Mickey Finn, my tutor,

RESEARCH LABORATORIES

The application of a scientific approach to control in brewing led to the arrival on the scene of consultant chemists – and then to brewing chemists. Which led Guinness to buy its first microscope in 1881 and to the appointment of its first consultant chemist, Alexander Forbes Watson, in 1895. He came in on a three-year contract at a salary of £500 a year (£35,000 in today's money).

From then on things developed fairly rapidly from the establishment of the Brewers' Laboratory in 1898 where routine checks were constantly carried out on raw materials. Guinness also got involved in the practical side of raw materials production when, in 1899, they paid the salaries and expenses (about £800 in all) of experts working on the growing of barley.

This was a project of educating Irish farmers by allocating small plots of land in different barley-growing areas dedicated to the production of various strains of barley. Farmers attended lectures in elementary agricultural science, soil, climate – all the basics that influenced barley growing. This whole operation was done in partnership with the fledgling Irish Agricultural Organisation Society founded in 1894 by the great Sir Horace Plunkett. The results of this work, plus the work done by a London consultant chemist called Horace Brown, resulted in the publication in 1903 of the first volume of *Transactions of the Guinness Research Laboratory*. After some internal debate involving the Board of Guinness, it was decided that this publication should be made available to the outside world and (a milestone decision) 'that for any scientific discovery we make which could not in any way be regarded as a trade secret we ought to communicate it to the world'. Guinness protecting and helping itself — and helping others.

Going on all the time in the Brewers' Laboratory there was, of course, the core work of constant monitoring of beer at its various stages in the brewing process. Then came the establishment of the Chemists' Laboratory in 1901 where research was to be done. Finally, in 1964, a splendid new laboratory was opened at St James's Gate. It has the imposing title of the Guinness Research Laboratory. The new laboratory had been specially designed to give the best possible facilities for modern research into the fundamental factors of brewing and provides the accommodation to house the equipment and staff of some sixty to carry out this objective.

In summary, this scientific endeavour at Guinness's has two main aims. One is to maintain and constantly strive to improve quality control over all materials used in the making of Guinness, over the process used in brewing it and over the saleability of the product itself as served to the consumer. The second is to continue as heretofore to play, and be seen to play, a leading role world-wide in industrial scientific research with particular relevance to brewing.

travelling to and from Abbey Street by bike. I usually shared these sessions with one or two students who were doing divinity in Trinity.

I visited the Naughtons fairly regularly and usually for Sunday lunch. That meant that I could do a couple of hours work with Mickey Finn on my way to or from Naughtons. Looking back on my self-imposed regimen it was tough — I was going to Mickey Finn two or three nights a week as well as at weekends. But I was young, healthy, fiercely ambitious — and utterly determined to succeed. I was unstoppable. I couldn't even stop myself!

Then, one day in September 1945, Mortier summoned me to his office. There he told me two things. One was that he had discussed my case with the Board of Directors and it had been decided that, in view of the fact that I had completed year one at Trinity, some arrangements should be made to allow me to attend all necessary lectures — *provided* I did it in my own time and did a normal day's work as well.

So Charles Mortier put it to me that I should be able to work out my Monday–Friday working week in term times by coming in on an early shift, breaking for some hours to attend lectures and laboratory work, and coming back to the Brewery to complete my eight-hour day. The second thing he told me was that, although I had just turned twenty-one and was now officially classified as a 'labourer', I was to continue indefinitely as a number-taker but be paid as a labourer. The difference was about £2 a week.

The details were easily worked out. The plan was formally authorised by Charles Mortier and all involved advised accordingly. And I became what was as near as no matter to being like any other undergraduate — except of course that an undergraduate in Trinity with a job of labourer must have been a little unusual in those days. True, I also had to work an eight-hour day which, during terms, left little time to do anything else — not even to sleep. But I enthusiastically and gratefully took up the gauntlet and I was off. It was a major breakthrough. And it was entirely due to my boss Charles Mortier. In my bumbling and naive way I tried to thank him. But he brushed me off affably and again he said — keep in touch. I did.

For the next three years my career did not change. I remained a number-taker. Most (if not all) of my butties joined the labouring list. They were given jobs at St James's Gate in various non-skilled capacities. Some racked casks. Some rolled casks. Some went for training as lorry drivers. Some donned uniforms and became gate porters or men

LORD MOYNE

When I worked in Internal Communications, in the 1970s, I had an office in a quiet corner of the Brewery, just beside the old St Patrick's Tower, and every now and again Lord Moyne (1905–92) would amble up the steps and ask if he could come in, telling me, as if I didn't know, that it said 'Internal Communications' outside. He would go on to remark that this seemed to be the right place to find out what was going on inside the Brewery. He gave the impression that he had blundered into the wrong office and didn't quite know why he was there, but he was Vice-Chairman of the Company, and behind that vague façade he had a fine grasp of detail.

Lord Moyne was a man of letters and he wrote plays and children's books. He had a wonderful old-world charm and he used to organise delightful soirées at his home in Knockmaroon (about three miles from the Brewery) at which there would be play-readings. He would select a play, decide on a date to read it, and invite the Guinness Players to organise a cast and to come and enjoy his hospitality. We would meet at St James's Gate from where the Guinness bus would take us to Knockmaroon. There we would sit around Moyne's drawing room, each with our part rehearsed, and off we'd go. Later our host would discuss the play and the author's work in general. At the end of the evening, we were invited to have a snack and some porter.

messengers. All were absorbed into the general pool of labour.

In Trinity, exams came and went. I remained on course. Outside term time I had opportunities to enjoy college life. From 1945 onwards men and women were coming back from the war and trying to settle down to learning on their education grants to get a degree of one kind or another – or to finish a course they were on before they went to war. Many of them gave up and left. Many persevered and did well.

Success

In April 1948 I did my degree exam. My subjects were Chemistry, Botany, Physics, Mathematical Physics. A few days later the results came out. I had passed. I went home with the news. The family reaction is easy to guess.

I went at once to see my boss and told him. I don't have to record his reaction. Joy unbounded. I went home again to discuss applying to Lever Brothers for a job, according to plan. In the early afternoon I was summoned to Charles Mortier – urgently. I found him in a state of great excitement. He was to take me straightaway to the Board of Directors. Walking to our assignation his main comments to me were that I should 'Be yourself'. No matter what happened I was to 'Be yourself'.

I was ushered into the boardroom by one of my ex-butties – a uniformed man-messenger. Directors stood, shook hands with me and offered congratulations about my degree. Then Lord Moyne talked to me about Dickens. Dr CK Mill (the MD and a scientist) asked me about my science course. Major-General Sir Charles Harvey (assistant MD and director in charge of personnel) asked me about my family and, in particular, about my father. AH Carlisle (assistant MD and ex-chief accountant) asked me if I'd ever considered a job in accountancy. I said I wouldn't like accountancy. Mortier was not invited into this conversation. He just sat there and listened attentively. Finally, Sir Charles thanked me for coming to talk to them and wished me well in my future career – wherever I went. I was very politely ushered out.

I came home and told my mother what had happened. Very interesting – but could we go back to talking about Lever Brothers and a job in Liverpool? About 4pm a bicycle-messenger arrived from Guinness. Mr Mortier wanted to see me urgently. Off I went on my bike and into the office of Charles Mortier. The scene that followed is the stuff of makebelieve. He literally threw his arms around me, congratulated me, and told me the Board had appointed me to the No. I Staff and I was to start next Monday.

A pause. It is said that one of the greatest moments in the life of any man or woman is when they win their first Olympic Gold Medal. Apparently no words can convey the extent of the thrill and the joy of that moment. The same is said of a woman at the moment of birth of her first child. The emotional feelings of euphoria are beyond description. It must be the same on receipt of a Nobel Prize.

That's why I'm simply unable to describe my reaction to being told this by Charles Mortier. Possibly the only thing I clearly remember is that when he kept on saying 'You did it! You did it!' I had the presence of mind to say 'We did it. We did it.' And I meant that. It would never have happened without both of us. I could, or can, never express my gratitude to that man. Meantime I'd just heard the unbelievable and everything was that bit out of focus.

As I left my boss's office, trying hard to steady myself, I walked down the stairs to shop-floor level. There, by sheer fluke, I bumped into my dad. He had just come up the Liffey, tied up the barge at the jetty, and was on the way to the tap for a well-earned pint. First I told him about getting my degree. He took my hand in an awkward, loving way — but couldn't say anything. Then I told him about being appointed to the No. 1 Staff. I said it clearly to him. But his only faltering, unnecessary, utterly human reaction was to ask me simply 'What staff?' I told him very briefly about the happenings of the day. He held my arm in his very strong, toil-worn hand. His eyes filled up. He said he'd see me soon at home. He was gone, off for his pint. In all, our meeting had lasted three or four minutes. He talked about it for the rest of his life. I'll never forget that precious incident.

Why had they offered me this job? Apart from the fact that the first Lord Iveagh was a graduate of Trinity, both the first and second Lords Iveagh became chancellors of Trinity College Dublin, and perhaps it seemed appropriate that the firm should find a staff job for a recent Trinity graduate among its own employees. Also, from the time Sir Charles Harvey took over as director in charge of personnel, the whole hierarchical personnel structure which had existed for almost two centuries had come under scrutiny. Quite correctly, Harvey decided that the whole thing had to be changed. The past was the past but the future was going to be very much different. And he was going to make those changes. My case could have been seen as an opportunity of demonstrating forthcoming changes.

Or it could have been that Lord Moyne had recalled the fact that (and I have only recently discovered this), according to the records, only two other Guinness people had succeeded in successfully combining a full-time job at St James's Gate with a full-time normal university course in Trinity College. In 1874 Christopher Digges La Touche came into Guinness as a management man. In his first few years in the Company he combined his work with a degree course in Trinity, where he graduated with a BA in 1878 and MA in 1880. And Edward Cecil Guinness, First Lord Iveagh, had done likewise. And here we were in 1948 with a kind of repeat case. Was I at long last being allowed the benefit of a precedent?

Or it just might be that the Board members had decided that anyone who had persevered over a long period in order to win a declared and commendable objective must have certain desirable qualities about them. This perceived determination to win through might well have impressed them — especially perhaps Harvey.

At any rate their decision was made and I was in. I had crossed the Rubicon. Barriers had collapsed. I was home and dry. On Monday 3 May 1948 I walked down the canal bank to St James's Gate. The word vertiginous occurs to me. My tangled thoughts bordered on the ridiculous. Was everybody aware of what was happening to me today?

As I discovered later, several interesting items did appear in the newspaper that day, though they were not about me. The weather forecast was for 'Fair periods. Some scattered showers. Rather cold.' (Wind had prevented a Water Wags race in Dún Laoghaire on the previous Saturday.) A Guinness Brewer, Guy Jackson, had won his Davis Cup match at Fitzwilliam and thereby put the Irish team two up against Luxembourg. The Dublin Grand Opera Society was putting on *La Bohème* at the Gaiety and Charlie Kuntz was opening at the Olympia (stalls three shillings and ninepence, circle two and six, gallery one and threepence). Newells of Grafton Street were advertising Gor-Ray skirts for two pounds and threepence, claiming that they were 'slenderising'. Dublin Gas Company workers returned to work after a strike and pork shops in Dublin were closed down by the police in an attempt to stamp out the black market in bacon. Under the heading 'Domestics Wanted' appeared the advertisement 'Active woman wants cleaning work. Short hours.'

But whatever about all that, I was walking boldly up the steps of the Front Hall at St James's Gate and the porter greeted me with 'Good morning, sir.'

The Trade Department

On day one of my first staff job I found myself attached to what was known as the Trade Department. The easiest way of describing the function of this department within the Guinness complex is to say that it acted as liaison between Guinness and almost anyone out there who bought or sold Guinness to anyone else. Of course there were dozens of strands to this operation but that's not a bad over-simplification.

Of primary importance to the department was its annual forecasts of how much Guinness would be needed to supply the estimated sales for the coming year. Our sales year started on 1 October and ended on the following 30 September. Three months before our sales year started, we had to estimate how much Guinness would be required every quarter, every month, every week of the forthcoming sales year.

And, based on our estimates, every other department at St James's Gate went into action organising what it would require to enable it to provide the right amount of whatever it was they provided – people, hops, malt, transport, heat, light, water, money, casks and so on. Collectively, then, the offices of the Trade Department were a hub of very interesting activities.

In order to learn about these various activities you had to spend some time in each section. I started in what was known as the Correspondence Office. We received a few hundred letters a day for our attention and a few hundred letters a day went out by way of replies. That meant that

MY DAYS IN THE WORLDS MOST FAMOUS BREWERY

there were plenty of letters to be composed. My apprenticeship in correspondence had started.

I shared a large office with one colleague. On our desk we had an internal and an external phone. By tradition, when your internal phone rang you picked it up and said just one word – your surname. When your external phone rang you picked it up and said 'Hello'. Using a very simple electronic technique there was a system whereby a member of the Board of Directors who wished to phone you simply picked up his phone and dialled your number. If your phone was disengaged you picked it up, identified yourself, and listened. But (and this was the clever gadget) if you were already engaged on your phone the call was cut off mid-stream and the Director announced himself and spoke to you. Very simple and very effective. Only Board phones had that facility.

Messengers were stationed in a small office outside our office and ready to be summoned by bells. They were responsible for keeping the office fire fed with fuel. And they changed your blotting pad and calendar every morning!

Lady Clerks

A constant stream of Lady Clerks came in to see you about one thing or another and to get your decision about action to deal with problems. As a class or category of personnel at the Brewery, Lady Clerks first made their appearance in 1900 when they took over various functions which were previously done by members of the No. 2 Staff. They

developed the use of typewriters for correspondence and also the use of shorthand when that became available. In 1953 there were 262 Lady Clerks on the books of the Company. Almost all of them were the product of good Irish schools and they were well-educated. For one reason or another, they had not gone ahead with third-level education but had opted instead for a secretarial career. On leaving school they had all completed a comprehensive, full-time course in what was called a 'commercial' college and had achieved certificates in competence in shorthand, typing, book-keeping, filing and so on.

When I first worked with them in 1948 they were highly intelligent and efficient. They were also very loyal to the Company. Some of them were in their late teens or early twenties. Some had been in the Brewery for many years. Because there was a rule that women had to resign on getting married, they were all single — except those who had at one time been in the Company, had married, and had been widowed and were thus allowed to take up employment again. In any case I addressed them as 'Miss' (or occasionally as 'Mrs', if they were widows). They all addressed me as 'Mr'. Very odd indeed. But I got used to it.

I have no way of knowing what kind of ratio of Catholics to Protestants existed among the Lady Clerks in 1953, but I think it fair to assume that, for a very long time after they first started coming into the Brewery, the majority came from Protestant schools and were therefore likely to be Protestant. Like admission to the No. I Staff, admission to the Lady Clerks staff included an interview. However, when my sister Mary applied for a job and was accepted, her religion was never mentioned nor did it hinder her in any way from doing very well.

The women in the Trade Department when I was there were all highly intelligent, efficient, jolly, fun-loving and a joy to work with, and I missed them when I went out on the road. I often wonder where they are now.

The daily round

As in most offices, there were very busy times and times when you had a quick look at the morning paper. A man came into the office once a week complete with a ladder and a small key. He was the clock winder. He spent his forty-four hours a week doing nothing else but winding Brewery clocks. Another man was employed for fixing typewriters. In a busy office there was always some machine that was misbehaving and he was on call to fix it.

There were no morning coffee breaks and no afternoon tea breaks. All staff, male and female, were normally on duty from 9am (sharp) to 4pm, except for those very senior ones who started at 10am. There were large ledger books for signing on and signing off. At 9.06am, the book was removed. If you arrived after that time there was nothing to sign but, by 11am, a note regarding your late arrival was delivered to your sectional boss and you had to explain yourself. When female and

THE GAU

It was the first Earl of Iveagh who, in 1925, laid the foundations for the Guinness Athletic Union by setting up a trust of £20,000 to buy three farms (total 17 acres) in Crumlin, on the outskirts of Dublin.

The GAU was the body established to administer and maintain Iveagh Grounds. In my time, the Executive Committee consisted of a representative from each of the dozen or more 'sections' (soccer, handball and so on) which meant that every section had a say in how the place was run. The Company supplied a member of the No. 2 Staff on the full-time job of Secretary of the GAU. In addition, the Company paid the wages of the people who worked in Iveagh Grounds – groundsmen, barmen and so on. And the Company also paid for the cost of maintenance and repairs.

Membership was confined to Guinness personnel and their families. You had the choice of paying your full yearly membership fee of ten shillings in one go – or you could have it deducted from your pay-packet at the rate of six pence per week. You could join as many sections as you liked – with a per-section fee of one shilling. There was a selection of games including soccer, rugby, hurling, gaelic football, men's and women's hockey, bowling, handball, cricket, tennis, boxing, badminton, swimming.

The GAU has always played an unobtrusive but very valuable part in the erosion of the personnel hierarchical structures within the Company. Out on the tennis court or on the soccer pitch nobody stops to ask what your job is before serving you an ace or before scoring a goal against you.

The La Touche Cup competition always had universal appeal. This was the annual, inter-departmental, soccer tournament for the trophy presented in 1906 by the then MD, Christopher Digges La Touche. It seemed that all departments participated. And all ranks of male personnel joined in. It ran for weeks. Modest bets were laid. Animated arguments went on. Home life was put aside. Iveagh Grounds became the meeting place of all and sundry. The La Touch Cup was to Guinness what the Sam Maguire Cup is to the GAA – and this competition still goes on. By that simple gesture all those years ago, La Touche has provided the object of endless fun, enjoyment and social intercourse. What a good sport he was!

The GAU is still alive and thriving, with a total of 3260 members. It is no longer confined to Guinness personnel – almost anyone can join – and Guinness Ireland has leased the Iveagh Grounds to the executive group who run it for a period of 21 years from 1994. The leasing fee is a peppercorn.

male staff reached a certain level of seniority they were excused from signing.

At the end of the working day, staff could sign off from 15.56 hours. That meant that, with a bit of luck, you could be gone on a bus, or in your car, or on your bike and be sipping tea in Bewleys or shopping in Grafton Street by 4.15pm. Or you could be knocking up on a tennis court in the Iveagh Grounds in Crumlin by 4.20pm. In winter, male staff could be playing squash on a staff court opposite the offices in James's Street just after 4.00pm.

Life as the 'hoofler'

Any male staff member joining the Trade Department automatically became the junior man to start with. He was known as 'the hoofler' – presumably from 'hoof' (in the sense of to kick). At any rate he was the lowest form of male staff in the department. It fell to him to do the myriad things that nobody else would do. For instance, if a female customer came into the downstairs cash office with a particular query which cashiers could not solve for her, the man messenger who looked after the Cash Office rang the hoofler to announce that there was a lady looking for him. This particular man messenger had been through World War I and was a great character. He explained to the hoofler (me) that the lady in question did not have a pram – so there was nothing to worry about!

Another duty of the hoofler was that he was in charge of the messengers – including men messengers. Dear, oh dear! What a turn-around. I had to supervise their weekly payout of wages. I also had to interview them about their attendance at the tech and issue warnings to those on the slippery slope. I paid out their cash awards for exams passed. And I had to operate a kind of one-man court martial for boys who were charged with misdemeanours such as slovenly appearance.

I also had to supervise the payout to Brewery widows who worked as office cleaners or who laundered the cloakroom roller towels. Many of these women were friends of my mother's and lived close by. And always they addressed me as 'sir' or 'Mr'. It was not that many years since these same women were giving out hell to me and my pals for banging a ball against their windows while playing football in our street with other brats.

I now took my lunch in the luncheon room marked 'No. 1 Staff'. (You will note the formal 'luncheon' rather than just lunch!) I couldn't afford a car and I decided (wrongly) that a bike was infra dig, so I walked to and from St James's Gate. I was using lavatories marked 'No. 1 Staff'. I was entitled to three weeks' leave. I was entitled to a 'Queen's Day' every year. (When Queen Victoria visited Ireland in 1849 the Board of Directors of Guinness decided to grant all 'commissioned officers' a day's extra leave every year from then on to commemorate the occasion.)

I got a bank account and a cheque book and my monthly salary was paid directly by Guinness into my bank account – nothing as sordid as actually handling cash! I had to go and see the manager of a nearby branch of the Royal Bank of Ireland to organise the opening of my bank account. He was a frightfully pompous little man, an ex-captain in the Royal Horse Artillery, whose approach was to make certain that this person opposite to him was actually 'suitable' to have an account in his bank. He was quite non-plussed to hear that my father had no bank account – anywhere!

When I went to the Medical Department to see a doctor I was treated by the chief medical officer, who addressed me as 'Mr Byrne'. Up till then I had been treated by a junior doctor and addressed as 'Byrne'. I was entitled to (and got) free supplies of oakwood shavings from the Cooperage Department for use as firelighters at home. They were actually delivered by Guinness van!

Protest and change

What happened next was interesting if for no other reason than that it shows the firm resistance, even up to 1948, to any changes in the normal appointment to the No. 1 Staff or to any changes in the personnel structures in the Company. It was a protest from some of them to my appointment. A small group went to see Sir Charles Harvey to express deep concern about the appointment of a labourer to their ranks. They pointed out that this might be seen by all as an erosion of their status and that of management in general – a situation that would militate against management control and might even affect the calibre of those from outside who might otherwise be very suitable for appointment.

The protest was thrown out – whether quietly or not I do not know. Harvey asked me to come and see him. He explained what had happened. No names were mentioned and I never found out who was involved, but he did say that I must not be surprised if some people showed their displeasure. It was almost bound to happen. And it was understandable. Nepotism would never be eliminated – it had its uses – but its great power had to make way to some extent to what he termed 'meritocracy'. He ended by saying that I was not to be surprised or upset. If things became nasty I was to come and see him about it.

But they never did. I didn't have to go back to him. On the whole, people were extremely nice to me. They grew to accept me and I learned to accept the situation and to be a bit sorry for those who felt bad about it. It wasn't their fault and it wasn't my fault that someone had got into the 'club' through a door that had been left slightly ajar and it was now too late to invoke 'blackball'. Only once or twice was there a barbed comment. I shrugged it off. I had to. Instead I just got on (as Charles Mortier told me to do) with 'being myself'. Whatever that was!

Then one day I was invited to come to a rehearsal of a play that was about to be put on by the Guinness Players. Why me? Well they thought I might enjoy it and that I might be persuaded to join the group and maybe do a bit of acting. They were right. I did enjoy the rehearsal. I did join the group. And I did some acting. And, although I didn't know it at the time, I would come to see that it was in the Guinness Players and other Brewery groups and societies that the real breakdown of personnel barriers within the Company was taking place in microcosm. The by-product of these organisations, whether it was intended or not, was that democracy among the personnel was going on – perhaps unbeknownst to and unnoticed by the very people directly and indirectly engaged in the change.

I moved from section to section within the Trade Department. My second stop was the Order Office which dealt with orders coming in from all over the country and also from the UK Guinness Stores and from European agents. It was the function of the Order Office to examine the order, check the financial standing of the customer and, all being well, to see that the beer was dispatched ASAP. Constantly throughout the day the other departments involved were kept advised about the following day's requirements. The Brewing Department had to know about the quantities of beer required; the Cooperage had to provide the casks; the Traffic Department had to organise transport; the accountants had to complete invoices and post them – and so on. But all this activity started with orders and although it was mostly routine stuff, now and again there was a crisis and that meant all hands on deck. That was challenging and exciting and when it was over we all settled down again to important but somewhat monotonous routine.

Grade A

Within a couple of years I was promoted to what was known as Grade B and stopped being the hoofler. The work I was doing became more responsible and I thoroughly enjoyed it. In 1954 I was further promoted to what was called Grade A and that meant that I was in line for a posting as a 'traveller' somewhere in Ireland. The thinking behind this system was very sensible. It centred around the axiom in the Trade Department that, 'If you want to get up you have to get out first.'

Translated, this meant that if, like me, you were assigned to the Trade Department, then you were dealing directly with the licensed trade and its members in Ireland. And the best way of finding out about what went on at pub level was to get out and into licensed premises and meet the people you might well be dealing with from the distance of HQ. You would get to know them better and understand the business from their point of view. It made good sense and, although I had no notion of where I might eventually be based or for how long, I knew that 'foreign' service was on the way and I would be exported sometime in the future.

Beginning journalism

When this waiting period started I decided on two things. One was that, while the work at St James's Gate was very interesting and at times challenging, I seemed not to be stretched and I wanted something else to do during my off-

THE GUINNESS PLAYERS

The Guinness Players started out in 1949 as the St James's Gate Drama Group. Later that group became the Guinness Players and, on the occasion of the formal opening of the Rupert Guinness Hall – a very large store which was converted at the Company's expense into a truly magnificent theatre for the use of all personnel – in 1951, it shared a double bill with the Guinness Choir. Players put on Sean O'Casey's *The Shadow of a Gunman*, and the choir did *Trial by Jury* by Gilbert and Sullivan.

I had the tiny part, in *Shadow*, of Mr Mulligan, the landlord of a Dublin tenement, where the peddler Seamus Shields was renting a room. My part was to come on stage in Shields's room and have strong words with him about his failure to pay the rent. My total time on stage was about four minutes but it was my first stage appearance and, in front of all the VIPs present, I had to do it well. The chap who played Shields was a real, true-blue Dubliner with a lot of stage experience. At rehearsals he demonstrated in no uncertain way his difficulty in remembering his lines but assured me that it would be 'all right on the night'. I followed the professional's practice of learning your own lines, plus those of your opposite number on stage. Anyway I came on stage and said my opening lines. I knew what he had to say but alas the words he said, though appropriate enough, were not those written by O'Casey. The next four minutes were truly awful for me. I was trying to say my lines in answer to cues never rehearsed! No words can describe my near-panic. The scene ended and I left the stage. The only reference to what happened was a word from 'Shields' that I had 'done well and had coped well with things'. Nobody else had noticed the mini-crisis. It taught me a lesson about stagecraft!

In the play *Ladies in Retirement* I played the part of a fly-by-night, irresponsible, young turk who was flirting outrageously with a young and pretty housemaid. The producer would have no awkward, modest, shillyshallying when it came to kissing – we would have to kiss 'convincingly' on stage. So we did. But the day after our 'first night' I was asked to have a word with one of my bosses who expressed the view that it was not exactly *comme il faut* to be kissing a girl on stage of an evening and expecting her to demonstrate the proper approach to her shorthand-taking with me next morning. We finished the run of the play (as produced) and I then had recourse to that age-old stratagem used by out-of-work actors – I rested. But only until the storm blew itself out.

The Players went from strength to strength and enjoyed very considerable success on the amateur drama circuit over the years.

duty time to absorb some of this unused energy. I had always wanted to write and I was now dictating letters to customers (and others) every day. But I wasn't quite satisfied with the quality or style of my writing and I wondered what to do about it.

The result of these misgivings was that my friend Frank and I took a decision. We signed on for a two-year correspondence course with the London School of Journalism. That proved to be a sound decision. We had to set aside a couple of evenings a week to keep us up with the course. We regularly received, by post, various practical tasks to do. They required research and that exposed us to interesting information and the system of finding it. We had to learn how to do it efficiently. After we had done our research, we were charged with writing articles of (usually) 750–1000 words on many subjects.

We submitted these for examination within the stipulated time and waited for our marking. This we got together with very helpful and useful comments and criticism. Awaiting our results we were like a pair of schoolboys. Almost always, Frank got marginally higher marks than I did and that set up a very healthy and positive competition between us as we followed our course – not to mention the odd bet or two. We learned a great deal about journalism – not only about the technique required for being a good journalist but also about the whole world of journalism and the journalist and how it all worked.

At any rate, we finished our two-year stint and were

awarded our certificates as graduates of the school. That was one good night! And although Frank was not really interested in submitting articles for consideration anywhere, we both believe he could easily have done very well. As for me, I found the course of great benefit to me in my job when it came to writing letters, submitting reports, researching particular histories of trade matters and so on. In my leisure time it also started me on the road to professional writing.

My second decision was that I should think about getting married.

Traveller

One day in 1956 my boss sent for me and told me I was being promoted to an appointment as 'traveller'. (The word 'representative' or 'rep' came years later.) I would be based in Cork. He explained that, as Cork was the HQ of two breweries, it was the area of greatest competition in Ireland in the selling of Guinness stout. He himself had been a Guinness traveller in Cork, so he was able to give me a valuable outline of what lay ahead of me. The Company would provide the Byrnes (I was married by then) with a Guinness house in Cork suburbia and arrangements would be made, at the Company's expense, for the transport of our goods and chattels and for re-furbishing the house we were going to live in.

Breaking the news to my wife, Frances, was not easy. She was working at the time as a biochemist on a team investigating the polio and 'flu viruses. They had laboratories in Montrose House – now the HQ of RTÉ. The series of experiments still had several months to go and she was obliged to stay on to the finish. So we did the only sensible thing – she stayed on in our Dublin flat and I checked-in to a Cork hotel and travelled to Dublin at weekends. Not the most felicitous way to celebrate the first year of marriage, but we really had little option. Because we were both on a five-and-a-half-day week I would leave Cork at noon on a Saturday and head for Dublin. I left again at about 5.30 on Monday mornings and reported for duty around 9am at the Cork store.

The Guinness traveller

A brief and over-simplified word about the role of a Guinness traveller. At the time there were five stores in Ireland – at Cork, Limerick, Galway, Sligo and Ballinasloe. The boss of each was called the store manager, and staff consisted of one or two No. 1 Staff, some Lady Clerks, one or two travellers and some labourers. The system was that there was a daily delivery by rail or barge of supplies from St James's Gate which were unloaded from the wagons or barges and kept in store under controlled conditions until the stout was ready for consumption. They were then delivered by road to the licensed outlets throughout the area by Guinness lorry or otherwise.

There were two travellers working out of the Cork store. One had the eastern half of Cork city plus east Cork county plus parts of Waterford and Kilkenny. I was assigned to the western half of Cork city, plus all of west Cork plus parts of east Kerry. Who could ask for a more attractive geographical area? Every second week I packed my traps and headed west, staying in various hotels on Monday to Thursday. Every other week I stayed in Cork city and worked around the inner areas.

Essentially the major job of a Guinness traveller was to see that our product was consistently presented to the consumer in top-class condition. This vital matter of preservation of quality was the principle first enunciated and practised by the first Arthur Guinness and it has been practised ever since by the Company. As it left the Brewery the quality was high. In rural areas it was nurtured in our stores and, as it left them, it was in superb condition. It was the job of the traveller to ensure that, on the last leg of the operation – publican to consumer – it was presented in a way that ensured consistent consumer satisfaction. But no product, no process, no handling of a product is always perfect. And, when it wasn't, it was our job to find out where things had gone wrong and to try and eliminate the cause.

That was the major function of a Guinness traveller. Next to that came what could be called customer service. That simply meant that we had to see to it that the services we were giving to our customers were good enough to allow him to present our product to the consumer in such a way that both he and the consumer were happy.

Looking back, our job on the road in Ireland was a real buzz. We called on pubs, clubs, restaurants and hotels – anywhere that Guinness was on sale. Wherever we went, we sampled Guinness both on draught and in bottle. We looked at the arrangements for cleaning the beer lines and beer taps. We examined the equipment used for bottling Guinness. We checked out the routine handling and stocking of our product – held too long and it might become too acid; not held long enough and it might not have the desired creamy head. Needless to say, everything wasn't always as it should have been and we had to explain to the customer that it was in his interests, besides ours, to keep things right. Local reputation for 'keeping a good pint' was an accolade not easily won but fairly easily lost, so it was something to be treasured. It meant good business. And we were there to help the publican to do good business. It was good for him and good for us. Team effort.

In the rural areas the Guinness traveller was often known in those days as the 'Guinness Inspector'. This goes back to the last century and the appointment of Guinness personnel as inspectors. Around 1880, Guinness had virtually no control of the way their product was handled once it left the Brewery. They had appointed two 'travellers' or 'collectors' and their job was to visit pubs in Dublin and collect the money owed to Guinness for supplies. But in 1890 it was discovered that publicans both in Ireland and in the UK were adding other beers, and sometimes water, to Guinness and selling it as pure Guinness. Since that was striking at the very heart of the success of Guinness — its high quality — something had to be done about it.

Enter what was then called the Guinness 'Travelling Officer', whose sole responsibility was to see to it that Guinness was not being adulterated. That led to the introduction of the famous Guinness trademark label on their bottled products, which was meant to guarantee that whoever bottled the Guinness, be it wholesaler or retailer, was legally committed to 'bottle no other brown stout'. Court cases followed for alleged breach of contract and Guinness had to follow a course of action which, while demonstrating their determination to see to it that their product as bought by the consumer was all it purported to

be and nothing less, nevertheless avoided any widespread condemnatinon of heavy-handedness from the licensed trade. Over time, they achieved their objective and the role of 'Travelling Officer' as guardian of the quality of Guinness became subsumed into a role in which, although it still contains to this day an important element of quality supervision, other aspects of the job have softened this one.

Because of this history, once we hit a town, unannounced, at ten o'clock of a morning, the news went around like wildfire and some tidying up was done just in time. If we were convinced that somebody was consistently failing to present Guinness as it should be presented, our final sanction (very rarely used) was that we should refuse to supply him. That was a serious step because it might deprive a man of his livelihood. But the consumer of our product deserved value for his or her money and it was part of our job to see that they got it.

Because we were in daily and close contact with our customers and, via them, with consumers, we got to know what was going on in the licensed trade in Ireland. We knew about what the opposition was up to and what influences, old and new, were affecting or likely to affect our sales. It was information-gathering that we all discussed among ourselves at our regular and frequent get-togethers.

On our calls we would offer some small items of advertising material (larger items had to be ordered) to help brighten up the pubs and to suggest a Guinness. These were things like ashtrays, dripmats, posters, showcards. We often found, though, that the more expensive type of ashtray was not on view on the counter where it should have been. The reason given was that it was reserved for use in the publican's own house because 'It's far too good for my customers'! Another reason given for its non-appearance was that, if it were put on the counter, it would be stolen.

We also might have a word about tardy payment of accounts or the overdue return of some empty casks. We tried not to create a situation which might embarrass the publican. When we went into a pub and had the usual exchange of pleasantries we bought a glass of draught and a bottle of Guinness. We had all done our tasting courses in the Brewery, so we went through the routine of taking the temperature of the stout, assessing its head retention and tasting it. All being well, we then discussed various items of business with the publican, shook hands, and left.

This routine was often carried out in the presence of a few locals in for a cure or an early morning pint to help them assess the day. When you left the place, the publican explained who you were and why you had called. And then the question often arose as to why you hadn't finished your drink. Was it because there was something wrong with it? Some of them were no longer sure that their own pint was OK. Maybe they should be given replacements? Anyway the result of all this little charade was that many a time a Guinness traveller found himself obliged to drink more than was good for him in order to keep a publican and his customers happy. In spite of this it was quite remarkable

how very few Guinness travellers eased down the slippery slope of having a problem with alcohol, but we often felt sorry for the chaps who had the far more difficult problem of representing hard liquor companies.

Another problem, but one which was almost entirely limited to the Cork area, was what was called 'mixing'. Stout produced by the local breweries, Murphys and Beamish & Crawford, was bought by publicans at a lower price than that at which they bought Guinness. That resulted in the price of a pint of Guinness being higher than a pint of local stout. In houses where the local stouts and Guinness were available it sometimes happened that when a consumer asked for a pint of Guinness he got a pint consisting of some Guinness plus some local stout. But he paid the price of a pint of Guinness – which meant that the publican made a little extra profit.

And this was done in spite of the fact that clearly marked casks of stout from all brewers were raised on stillions at the back of the bars in Cork for the consumers to see. Was this petty? Well, perhaps. But it can be argued that such attempts to sell the local stouts instead of Guinness was actually part of the admirable and fierce local loyalty which Corkonians have for their city and everything about it. In a very practical way this loyalty makes great sense. Beamish & Crawford dates back to 1792 (only thirty-three years younger than Guinness) and Murphy's brewery was founded in 1856. Over all those years, these two breweries have provided jobs for heaven knows how

Continued on page 147

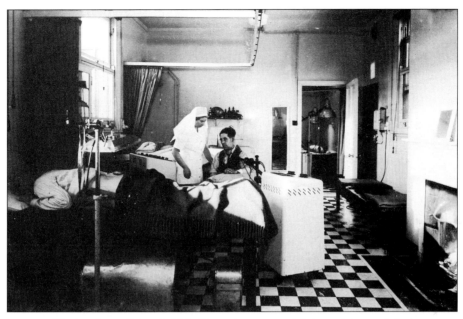

The physiotherapy clinic in the Medical Department was one of the first such clinics in Ireland.
All personnel plus their families were entitled to come for treatment free of charge.

The pharmacy of the Medical Department c 1945, complete with jars, weighing scales and Dickensian high stools

The stage is all set in the Rupert Guinness Hall for yet another production by the Guinness Players. Since 1949 this group has won many prizes for its productions at drama festivals all over Ireland.

The famous Guinness trademark device which was registered in 1876 is based on the O'Neill or Brian Boru Harp — the earliest Irish harp known to us and the oldest in existence, now in the Library of Trinity College, Dublin.

The Guinness Choir — one of the most distinguished and
talented groups ever formed at St James's Gate. Its repertoire
over the years is highly impressive and the continuous plaudits
heaped upon it are well earned.

The late Cathal Gannon at his
keyboard. This Guinness carpenter
has left his mark on Irish musical
history. The Company and his
many friends and colleagues are
very proud of him.

Judging exhibits at 'the Fanciers' show

At the annual 'Fanciers' in the Iveagh grounds there was all the fun of the fair.

Because of the acute shortage of housing at the end of World War II, the Company provided the capital to build a housing estate at Terenure (a few miles from St James's Gate) and then organised attractive mortgage facilities to enable Guinness personnel to buy the houses.

Desk-bound days in my career

'Lest We Forget'
Every year Guinness personnel from St James's Gate who were on active service during World War II
attend memorial services in Dublin churches and here at the Irish National War Memorial at
Islandbridge on the Liffeyside.

BOARD OF DIRECTORS.

NAME.	RANK.	REGIMENT.	DECORATION.
Elveden, The Viscount, C.B., C.M.G., M.P.	Captain ...	... Royal Naval Volunteer Reserve	A.D.C. to H.M. the King, 1916—1918
Guinness, The Honble., W. E., M.P.	Lieut.-Colonel	... The Duke of York's Own Loyal Suffolk Hussars	Distinguished Service Order and Bar. Mentioned in Despatches three times.

ACCOUNTANT'S DEPARTMENT.

NAME.	RANK.	REGIMENT.	DECORATION.
Atkinson, C. B. ...	... Sub-Lieutenant	... Royal Naval Volunteer Reserve (Auxiliary Patrol)	—
*Birmingham, W. A.	... 2nd Lieutenant	... 6th Royal Irish Fusiliers ...	—
Bright, H. S. ...	... Captain ...	... Machine Gun Corps	Military Cross. Mentioned in Despatches twice.
Hill, C. L. ...	... Lieutenant ...	... Royal Field Artillery	—
Middleton, A. H.	... Lieutenant ...	... Royal Munster Fusiliers ...	—
Troy, D. F.	... Sergeant ...	... Royal Army Medical Corps ...	—
*Ward, B. L. ...	... Corporal ...	... 2nd Royal Dublin Fusiliers ...	—

AUDIT DEPARTMENT.

NAME.	RANK.	REGIMENT.	DECORATION.
Burkitt, R. F. ...	... Major ...	... Royal Garrison Artillery (S.R.)	Military Cross.
Clarke, P. B. C. ...	... 2nd Lieutenant	... 11th Royal Dublin Fusiliers	
Fisher, C. G. C. ...	... Captain ...	... Royal Dublin Fusiliers ...	Military Cross.
Holland E. F. J. ...	... Lieutenant ...	... 9th Royal Irish Rifles ...	Military Cross.
Kelly, G. W. ...	... Captain ...	... Royal Army Service Corps	—
Macnie, W. R. ...	... Lieutenant ...	... 5th Royal Irish Fusiliers	
Moorhead, J. F.	... Captain ...	... Royal Army Service Corps	—
Wood, N. ...	... Sergeant ...	... 7th Royal Dublin Fusiliers ...	—

BREWHOUSE DEPARTMENT.

NAME.	RANK.	REGIMENT.	DECORATION.
Armstrong, Edward	... Lance-Corporal	... 1st Irish Guards...	—
Bannister, E. C. ...	... Lieutenant ...	... Royal Army Service Corps ...	—
*Bligh, Thomas ...	... Guardsman...	... 2nd Battalion Coldstream Guards	—
*Boland, John ...	... Sergeant ...	... 2nd Irish Guards	—
Bowyer, P. G. ...	... 2nd Lieutenant	... 5th City of London (London Rifle Brigade)	—
Brien, Michael ...	... Staff-Sergeant	... Royal Army Medical Corps ...	—
Brien, William ...	... Gunner ...	... Royal Field Artillery	—

* Killed in action or died of wounds.

Page from the Roll of Honour book which contains the names of all the Guinness personnel who fought in World War I. They are recorded in the book under department and then alphabetically rather than by rank. Asterisks denote those who were killed in action or died of their wounds.

COOPERAGE DEPARTMENT *(continued)*.

NAME.	RANK.	REGIMENT.	DECORATION.
Daly, Thomas	Trooper	1st Life Guards	—
Delaney, Edward	Sapper	Royal Engineers	—
Delaney, Joseph	Lance-Corporal	2nd Royal Irish Rifles	—
Doyle, John	Private	6th East Lancs.	—
Doyle, Patrick	Trooper	4th Hussars	—
Dunne, Patrick	Sapper	Royal Engineers	—
Dunne, Stephen	Private	Royal Army Service Corps (M.T.)	—
Dunphy, Patrick	Gunner	Royal Garrison Artillery	—
Farrelly, Patrick	Sergeant	3rd Royal Irish Fusiliers	—
*Foran, Thomas J.	Private	Royal Army Medical Corps	—
*Foster, John	Rifleman	1st Royal Irish Rifles	—
Fox, Patrick	Guardsman	2nd Irish Guards	—
Gogarty, Francis	Acting-Corporal	Royal Army Medical Corps	—
Halford, Francis	Corporal	Royal Army Medical Corps	—
Hanlon, Peter	Sergeant	8th Royal Irish Fusiliers	—
*Heffernan, Martin	Private	9th Royal Dublin Fusiliers	—
Hegarty, Joseph	Private	Royal Army Medical Corps	—
Helly, John	Steward	Naval Sick Berth	—
Hendrick, Patrick J.	Gunner	Royal Garrison Artillery	—
Hill, Joseph	Corporal	Royal Engineers	Distinguished Conduct Medal. Military Medal.
*Hoare, Joseph	Guardsman	1st Irish Guards	—
Hogan, Joseph	Private	Royal Army Medical Corps	—
Hogan, Michael	Private	2nd Batt. Royal Dublin Fusiliers	—
*Hopkins, James	Private	8th Royal Dublin Fusiliers	—
Joyce, Augustine	Sapper	Royal Engineers	—
Kavanagh, Thomas	Trooper	4th Hussars	—
Keeble, Albert	Sergeant	1st Wiltshire Regiment	—
Kelly, Michael	Private	21st Royal Scots Fusiliers	—
Kelly, Michael	Corporal	Royal Irish Regiment	—
*Kerr, William	Private	Royal Army Medical Corps	—
King, Charles	Corporal	26th Batty. Royal Field Artillery	—
Lacey, Edward	Guardsman	1st Irish Guards	—

* Killed in action or died of wounds.

Page from the Roll of Honour book

Continued from page 138

many Cork people. And that means a good living for countless thousands of families. Small wonder then that local Cork people have supported local employers – and, besides, the products they produce are worthy opposition for Guinness.

Guinness first established its store in Cork in 1891. Since then it has operated in what, in sales terms, is alien (or at least hostile) territory. But our sales have always been buoyant and relations with the two opposition brewers have always been cordial and civilised. Competitive, yes, but adult and proper.

Settling in Cork

After a few months, my wife's contract in Dublin was completed. She moved down to Cork and we got a house on the western outskirts of the city. One of our close neighbours was a member of the Murphy brewing family, and we got on very well. Also, I played squash in the army barracks in the city and found myself in the company of one or two Murphy executives. After play, we swapped pints in a local hostelry and agreed that, while it was relatively easy to distinguish Beamish & Crawford stout from Murphy's or Guinness, it was not always easy to distinguish between Murphy's and Guinness. When we got around to mixing the stouts in the same glass and trying to identify the mixture we decided it was time to go home!

My sojourn in Cork produced an unexpected pleasure for me. My bailiwick as a traveller included a small village in the far west of Cork called Allihies. It was once a thriving copper-mining area but the mine was now defunct. There was growing hope of a re-opening and the prospect made the locals very excited. I was interested in this story and wrote an article on it, which was published in *The Irish Times* a few days later. It was my first time in print in an Irish daily.

As within St James's Gate so it was outside in the trade – the question of religion came up. When I went on the road in 1956, four out of five of our store managers were Protestant. Almost all of the store staff were Protestant. And at least 85% of all Guinness travellers were Protestant. As far as the males were concerned, the reason for this was that male posts out in the trade, in stores or as traveller, were normally filled by members of the No. 1 Staff and, since almost all of these were Protestant, it followed that the majority of male store staff and travellers were Protestants.

Did this matter? Or, more to the point, did this affect our sales in any way? Who can possibly say? And, since well over 90% of Guinness publicans in Ireland and over 95% of Guinness drinkers in Ireland were Catholic it was not irrelevant to be asking these questions. Certainly this matter never occurred to me until I went on the road and a publican here or there would comment that 'Byrne is not exactly a Protestant name to be representing Guinness.' There is no doubt whatever that our customers had fine and healthy respect for Guinness personnel. They often referred to a Guinness traveller as 'the Guinness gentleman' – and they behaved as gentlemen, too. The publican always knew that he was dealing with an honourable company with honourable personnel. But if you ask did they actually *like* the Guinness traveller then that's another matter.

While we lived in Cork, we joined the Ashton Players, a local drama group based in the (Protestant) Cork Grammar School, which put on many of the Yeats plays locally and competed in various drama festivals in Ireland. We came to see our families in Dublin and Drogheda about every second weekend. And we discovered the beauties of the west Cork/east Kerry landscape.

Move to Galway

We were just settling in to our enjoyable life amid Cork people when I was transferred to Galway. A trade problem had arisen there and I was told I was being sent there as a kind of troubleshooter. And so it was that on a summer's day in 1957 we arrived in Galway, where we lived for three years.

Galway is a wonderful place, and from beginning to end it was sheer joy and we loved it. It's grown and changed now, but we had the great good fortune to see it at its wonderful best. We lived in a Guinness house out at Salthill. It was a large, old house on two acres of raised land with clear views of Galway Bay and County Clare. The house itself was magnificent but needed some major repairs because of dry rot. While we lived there, the Company

decided to knock it down but, before they did that, they built a new house on the tennis court and we moved in.

Guinness had a very attractive western HQ just off Eyre Square. Staff consisted of a store manager, one traveller (me), three Lady Clerks and some three or four labourers. Railway wagons from St James's Gate came into the store every day, were off-loaded, loaded with empties, and went back to Dublin. From the store, Guinness was delivered to customers all over County Galway, parts of County Mayo and parts of County Clare. My bailiwick or 'travelling district' covered more or less the same area as the goods delivered from the store. That introduced me to the joys of Connemara, south Mayo and north Clare and that is scenery not to be surpassed anywhere.

As it had been when I worked in the Cork area, we Guinness travellers in the Galway area were not salesmen in the sense that Guinness reps today are salesmen. We did not take orders or money from publicans and we were not responsible for their competence in keeping their stocks right – except to ensure that under- or over-stocking did not lead to Guinness being sold in less than top condition. We were not responsible for installing or maintaining or cleaning their beer lines (beer travelling from cask to glass), but we were involved in dealing with the likely result of inadequate attention to beer-lines, in other words, the state of our stout as served to the consumer. And we had a duty to see that relationships between all our customers and the

Company were in good shape and that our combined efforts were working to our mutual satisfaction.

Visiting the Aran Islands

Part of the job of the Galway-based Guinness traveller was to visit the three Aran Islands at least every three months and to call on all licensed premises on Inishmore, Inishmaan and Inisheer – a total of some ten pubs. The routine was that you boarded the coaster *Naomh Éanna* in Galway Docks at 8am and set off across Galway Bay for Inishmore. As it happened, the captain of the vessel had been in the merchant navy during World War II and had been through the hell of the shipping lanes in the North Atlantic. He was a great character with many a story to tell. He insisted that I should use his cabin on my voyages.

At the time there was a weekly spot in *The Irish Times* called 'Profile'. Every Saturday they picked interesting people and gave them a write-up with a picture. I organised a picture to be taken of the captain at the helm and I wrote a thousand words about him. When it was published he was delighted. So was I – mostly because it gave a little showing to an unsung hero. On my next trip to the islands we spliced the mainbrace on the way home!

Having done most subjects at school through Irish, my Irish was quite good, so on my first trip to the Aran Islands, I greeted the publican in the first pub I came to in Irish and continued to hold a conversation with him in that language. The man was flabbergasted when he discovered who I was,

since it was the first time that 'the Guinness man' had spoken in Irish to an Aran Island publican. Well, we drank to that!

The routine for visiting the island pubs was that we went direct from Galway to Inishmore. There we stayed for some time while passengers disembarked and goods were off-loaded. There were no cars on the island and the Guinness traveller hired a horse-drawn hackney to allow him to do his rounds of the pubs. Back then to the jetty and off we chugged to Inishmaan, where the same routine went into action. And so to the last and smallest of the three islands – Inisheer. In those days there was no suitable jetty at Inisheer so the *Naomh Éanna* had to drop anchor off-shore where we were met by a veritable flotilla of currachs (coracles). We watched while sheep and cows were lifted in slings from steamer to currachs and rowed ashore. That done, it was the turn of passengers to leave the steamer by gang-way into a currach and lusty sinews rowed us ashore. Again the Guinness traveller found his way by single horse-power to the pub and did his business. Again the publican was intrigued to meet the first Irish-speaking Guinness traveller 'in the nearest pub to America'. The first time I did this trip I felt like a latter-day Stanley where I would not have been all that surprised to see Dr Livingstone sitting, Guinness in hand, in one of the Aran Island pubs.

Then it was back by currach to the steamer and back to the jetty at Inishmore to collect passengers and load freight. As arranged, I popped into the first pub to say *slán* to my new-found friend the publican. I was taken into the kitchen to meet his wife and to have tea before sailing for Galway. Being invited into a kitchen in rural Ireland is a far greater compliment than being invited into the parlour. The parlour is for visitors like the parish priest. The kitchen is for relatives, family, neighbours — and friends. His wife it was who brought up the question of an Irish-speaking Guinness traveller and asked 'And are you a Catholic too?' The question whether Guinness was 'at last going to employ Catholics' came up and required appropriate handling.

As I left, my friend told me that he had left a small parcel of lobsters for me on board the steamer and that, even as he was telling me, they were being boiled in sea water in the galley and would be cooked by the time we got to Galway. And indeed they were. So ended a memorable day for me.

On all subsequent visits I was treated extremely well by all the island publicans and doing business under such conditions was a real pleasure. I smiled at the thought that I was actually being paid for doing it!

There was one other thing about the Aran Islands which I'll never forget. It was while I was on one of my visits that I learned by phone that I had become a father. Our first child, a daughter, Hilary Emer, had been born early that morning in hospital in Drogheda where my wife had been staying with her mother for the few days leading up to the birth. Knowing that the great event was about to happen did not prepare me for the shock. I suspect I told

VISITING UCG

Guinness staff members always made a habit of involving themselves with local people, wherever they found themselves, and so it happened that one Saturday, by arrangement, I visited University College Galway to see the place and to write an article about it for *The Irish Times*. To my great delight I was greeted by the President of UCG, Monsignor Paddy Browne. This was the legendary scholar and translator also known as Monsignor Pádraig de Brún whose greatest claim to fame is probably his translation of Homer's Odyssey which adapts the Homeric metres to Irish rhythms thereby displaying a quite remarkable ability to capture the freshness and immediacy of the Greek narrative. He called this work *An Odaise*. My trip around UCG with that man as guide is something never to be forgotten. Nor is the chat in his study which followed — complete with a bottle and two glasses. The article was published in *The Irish Times* and elicited considerable interest.

every publican on the islands about the event and it was the second time that the mainbrace was spliced on the trip back home to Galway!

The Oyster Festival

Like all Guinness staff, I took an interest in local matters wherever I went, but the Guinness involvement in the Galway Oyster Festival is quite a different sort of local involvement. This festival started off in 1954 with a tiny squeak which eventually got so loud that it was heard locally, nationally and internationally. The Galway Chamber of Commerce had decided to do something to boost the profits of local pubs, restaurants, hotels and shops by enticing more visitors to Galway. That led to thinking about indigenous food and drink to go with it. And that led to oysters and Guinness. A tiny band of some two dozen local stalwards (including the Guinness store manager) went off to a pub in Clarenbridge (about ten miles from Galway city) and, one Saturday at the beginning of September 1954, they celebrated the start of that year's harvesting of local oysters. And, as they say, the rest is history.

When I arrived in Galway in 1957 I was promptly conscripted on to the Galway Oyster Festival Committee. The venture was still in its infancy but, among other things, it marked my introduction to major Guinness promotions and the rationale of our involvement in such things. There were at least two good reasons for the Guinness involvement in the Oyster Festival and such considerations have remained to this day among the major criteria as to why the Company gets involved in promotions.

It was seen by us as a means of generating more sales and more profits. Also, involvement in any scheme to entice more tourists locally is something a company like Guinness should look at because more tourists mean more spending and we are potential beneficiaries of such spending.

It is commonly agreed that for the last fifty years or so, oysters have been the food of people with enough money to be able to afford them – in other words, they are expensive. So the notion of Guinness with oysters is aimed at a fairly well-heeled sector of the community and its not often that Guinness gets an opportunity of aiming at such people. And of course, oysters and Guinness go well together anyway.

Besides all this we were supporting a truly festive occasion, which has always drawn a lot of local, national and international publicity which more than justified the cost to us of the promotion. The very attractive pageant of the Oyster Queen arriving by boat from the oyster beds and presenting the first oysters of the season to all and sundry makes for excellent television coverage. By now, this festival accounts for the spending of a considerable amount of money in the Galway area and also for the consumption of 100,000 oysters and countless thousands of pints of Guinness!

Hunting and clubbing

In my twenties I learned to ride horses. I was 'schooled' both in Ireland and in the UK. When I came to live in Galway it was an opportunity to sample hunting. So I had some outings with the Bermingham & North Galway Hunt

151

and with the Galway Blazers. Hunting is a winter sport and, since I worked a five-and-a-half-day week, I had little time for keeping riding-fit in the short days of winter. I soon realised that, generally speaking, the people who hunted were not so short of keeping-fit time during the week and indeed they mostly hunted several times a week. All of this meant that it was impossible to keep fit to hunt, and to do so without being fit was courting trouble. So, reluctantly, I had to stop hunting.

I was invited to join the Galway County Club. I was delighted to accept that invitation and I met a great cross-section of people there, all male, from their twenties to their eighties, with all kinds of occupations – business, manufacturing, academic, professions – retired, idle rich, locals, overseas, blow-ins. (The Galway expression for someone who has come to live in Galway from outside the west of Ireland is to say that 'He came in the Oranmore Road.' Like jazz, if you have to have that explained to you, better just ignore it!)

They had a very curious game at the club, which was played on a billiards table with the same number of balls as used in snooker and which they called 'splosh'. Nearly all members entered for the Christmas competition which had turkeys as prizes, and side betting for those who were so inclined. It brought out the very best in all of us by way of sheer enjoyment and laughter.

SALMON AND GUINNESS

You might well wonder what the connection is. Is this some new recipe? Or is there a move afoot to persuade salmon to drink Guinness on the grounds that it's good for them?

The truth is that an organisation called the Salmon Research Trust of Ireland was established in 1955 jointly by the Minister for Agriculture and Guinness. Its main aim was to try to find out more about the sea-life habits of salmon. For instance, whereabouts in the ocean do salmon go? Why do some salmon remain at sea for two or three years while others return after one year? Are these factors determined by heredity or environment or both or neither? What are the survival rates in the sea after spawning? Is the fish population of a given river more influenced by the chemical nature of its water or by its vegetation? How do weather, water temperature and flow affect fish movements?

But what has all this to do with Guinness? Well, for one thing, the answers to such questions are an important contribution to scientific knowledge. Secondly, these answers must lead to an increased knowledge of a product which is the backbone of a valuable national industry – the fishing industry. There is also the tourism business to consider. Fishing in Ireland has always been, and remains, a considerable draw for home and overseas fishing folk and that in turn generates sizeable income for the country. Lastly the work involved in this project has produced quite a number of jobs. What's good for Guinness is good for Ireland. What's good for Ireland is good for Guinness. Scientists and others would rate it as a good example of business mutualism!

For a variety of sensible reasons the marriage, so to speak, between the Ministry of Agriculture and Guinness was dissolved in 1989 and the whole operation at Newport, Co Mayo, passed over to the Department of Fisheries. From 1998 it came under the umbrella of the Marine Institute – the government organisation responsible for the co-ordination and promotion of marine research and development. In the dissolution, Guinness handed over as a gift the very valuable premises and plant at Newport to those who are continuing the good work going on up there which, among other benefits, is now being shared with Ireland's partners in the European Union.

More journalism

Although I enjoyed my life in Galway, the routine work of visiting an average of fifteen pubs a day was not intellectually stretching. I felt that I was driving in second or third gear. I had to do something to use up my surplus energy. I had been doing some radio work for RTÉ, and now I did more of it. This resulted in weekend trips to Dublin, which allowed me to visit my mother (my father had died by this stage) and go on to Drogheda to see my in-laws. I was also writing more stuff for newspapers and, as always, reading a lot.

Moving to Ballina

Some Guinness travellers had an immediate boss such as a store manager and some were 'independent' – in other words, having served for some years attached to a store or to HQ in the Dublin area, they had been promoted to being off on their own somewhere in rural Ireland where they were directly responsible to the big boss in Dublin, the trade manager. When I say 'promoted', I do not mean that it necessarily included a salary increase, but it meant that you lived in a Company-owned house which you also used as your office. Communications with HQ was done mostly by post but sometimes by phone.

In autumn 1960 I was informed that I was being promoted from store traveller to independent and was moving from Galway to Ballina, Co Mayo. To put it mildly, we were shattered. We were extremely happy in Galway and our three years there had given us the time to settle down. And now this move. Promotion – yes, but at what domestic cost? It meant that within five years, we lived in five houses (one in Dublin, one in Cork, two in Galway and now one in

Ballina). Not easy. But then you remembered that one of the clauses in your agreement to accept an appointment to the No. I Staff was that you agreed to serve the Company 'wherever you were required to do so'. Fair enough. You kept to your agreement or you took the alternative.

The Guinness house in Ballina was modern and spacious on about an acre of land and with a very pleasant view overlooking the River Moy. With regrets at leaving Galway, we settled in and my job did not change – except that I was on my own and free to operate my assignment more or less as I wished. Hence 'independent'. But I learned that this new-found independence actually resulted in being more disciplined than when I had had a local boss.

Social life in Ballina was restricted There were no theatres, there was no squash court, and we were not interested in fishing or golf. And so most weekends we headed east to see our families or they came and stayed with us. We made a few friends and we produced our second child – this time a boy, named Ian Edward. Joy unbounded. It was a period of quiet and pleasant living. But it was not like Galway.

Because I had an office in the house, I was my own secretary. This included dealing with the contents of the daily letter from HQ and the preparation and dispatching of my daily letter to them. I had quite a bit of typing to do and I was very glad to have done a typing course as part of my training on the journalism course.

I became involved with a local group. The local Pioneer

Total Abstinence Association, who were dedicated to the principle of not drinking alcohol, had decided to put on a Christmas pantomime and asked me to produce the show, to which I gladly agreed. Of course the inevitable happened. The news that 'the Guinness man' was producing the Pioneer panto spread around the area and created quite a stir. It was a great source of fun and banter with some of my customers and the whole episode made for easier social relationships between town people and Byrnes. Eventually the show ran to packed houses for several nights and one of its most applauded moments was when there was a skit on stage which centred around a huge Guinness advertisement.

During my time in Ballina an incident occurred which was to make a major difference to me in my future career both within and outside the Guinness organisation. I was on my rounds one morning in Belmullet and, as I entered a pub, the proprietor, a particularly nice man with whom I had had many an interesting chat, was reading that morning's newspaper. 'I see here that your boss has retired,' he remarked, and he showed me the announcement that Lord Iveagh had retired as Chairman and had handed over to his grandson.

I was very surprised, not just at the retirement itself, but at the realisation that it took a customer to tell me about an important happening in my Company. It was an example of very defective communications on the part of the Company that front-line troops such as travellers were not kept *au fait* with matters which merited media coverage about the Company. I was very annoyed about that. And I vowed that if ever I found myself in a position to see to it that such things didn't happen again I would try very hard to do something about it. The day after my embarrassing conversation with the publican, and the day after the anouncement appeared in the papers, I found, inside my letter from HQ, a letter marked 'Strictly Private and Confidential', to tell me that Lord Iveagh had retired!

By the time we had spent almost a year in Ballina, we had decided that we didn't want to stay there for ever. There was nothing wrong with Ballina or its people. It was simply that we weren't suited to life there, and so we looked to ways out. We were both in our middle thirties. As a biochemist with a fair amount of research experience and achievement, Frances could get a job in Ireland or the UK or America, and I could probably get a job in broadcasting or as a journalist.

The first step was to make diplomatic enquiries at HQ about the likely length of our posting in County Mayo. No joy there: 'It could be a matter of weeks or months or years,' they told us. I never thought I'd see the day when the idea of leaving Guinness would strike me, but we didn't want to stay on indefinitely in Ballina, and in any case, I was finding that my work kept me in second gear and that was not something which would make anyone happy.

Two other things happened which suggested that there might well be a market for our talents elsewhere. I visited my brother in St Louis, Missouri, and he took me to see the local massive Anheuser-Busch brewery, where I met several executives – including the big boss himself. The day after my visit I was invited to meet one of the people I met on my tour and he explained to me that, within the year, they would be opening a new brewery in Florida, and they offered me a very attractive job in marketing/sales. They gave me a month to consider the offer.

The second offer, of an attractive job with an international brewing company operating in Ireland, came out of the blue. That was a real shocker because, amongst other things, acceptance might easily be construed as disloyalty to Guinness on their home ground and that was something which, up to then at any rate, was anathema to me.

So we thought and talked about it all. Then one day logic came to my aid. Out in the wilds of the Erris peninsula I had a blinding flash of the obvious. Suppose that instead of the Byrnes moving away from the Guinness station in Ballina, the station itself should be removed? That would leave the Byrnes without a base from which to operate and might well result in repatriation to Dublin. But who would buy that notion? I worked for weeks on my proposition that, strictly from the Guinness point of view, there was no justification, either financial or trade or otherwise, in maintaining a base in Ballina. The whole thing could be done more effectively and at a far lesser cost from Sligo.

The details of the case are too tedious to enumerate

here. I did a report on it and sent it to HQ. It was accepted. We were instructed to negotiate the sale of the house in Ballina and we were to return to Dublin within a month or two. And so, in the autumn of 1962 we arrived back to a small flat in Sandyford in County Dublin.

Advertising

There is a story that goes like this. Two men are out for a stroll, and the first man says, 'You know that Guinness poster?'

The second man replies, 'The one with the bird with the absurdly long beak – what do you call it? – a toucan? Yes, that's it, a toucan. With a great yellow beak and some kind of rhyme under it – something about Guinness is good for you and ending up "just see what toucan do". Terrible pun.'

'Yes,' says his friend, 'that's the poster I mean. Have you seen it?'

'No,' says the second man, 'I never look at advertisements.'

It's a strange thing about Guinness and advertising, but the two are almost as inextricably linked as Guinness and goodness, and whether they like it or not, virtually everyone is aware of it. At least that is one of the things I found out when I decided to investigate Guinness advertising because advertising was a major weapon in my armoury in my job in sales. Guinness advertising has always been and remains even today a hotly debated subject, in pubs and clubs and anywhere people are having a drink. It is an institution. It has never stopped moving and over the seventy years of its existence, it has retained that quirkiness which is summed up neatly as its Guinnessness.

Guinness began professional newspaper advertising in 1929, when it took advertising space in the *Daily Chronicle*. The message was unambiguous. It said, 'As a result of quality, and quality alone, the Guinness Brewery has grown to be by far the largest in the world.'

The first Guinness slogan, as practically every sentient person knows, was the straightforward message 'Guinness is Good for You'. Apart from pub showcards, the first time substantial Guinness advertising appeared in Ireland was when that slogan appeared on Dublin buses in 1951.

Then came the pelican, with seven pints of Guinness balanced on its beak and accompanied by this verse:

A wonderful bird is the pelican
Its bill can hold more than its belly can
It can hold in its beak
Enough for a week
I simply don't know how the hell he can.

Next came the ostrich and the glass of Guinness in its neck, apparently the wrong way up. That was followed by a flood of letters from the public, but the artist John Gilroy, who designed the poster and created the Guinness-guzzling animals, had a reply all ready. He said that the ostrich had been imitating the sea-lion by balancing the glass on its nose. It had then flicked it up into the air, opened its beak and the glass had gone down the easiest way, to be properly enjoyed in its stomach. Twenty years later came this comic verse:

The ostrich, many people think
Has never learned the way to drink
They say the goblet, glass or cup
Is going down the wrong way up

And Guinness that you cannot taste
Is so much Guinness gone to waste.

Then, in 1935, came the toucan mentioned earlier, probably the most famous of the Guinness birds. It was Dorothy Sayers (the crime-writer) who wrote the verse that went with it, for at the time she did some copywriting for an advertising agency:

If he can say as you can
Guinness Is Good for You
How grand to be a toucan
Just think what toucan do.

Another John Gilroy poster was the one showing a man carrying what is obviously a very heavy girder. Gilroy's son, an engineer, apparently pointed out to his father that the girder in the draft drawing was placed in a position that couldn't possibly balance, and so Gilroy senior had to redraw the illustration. As things turned out, the poster was an absolute triumph – to the point that people ordering Guinness in pubs in the UK started asking for a girder, and people applying for jobs in the Company were told that the first test of their suitability would be to see if they could pick up and carry a girder.

At one time, Guinness took advertising space in some of the British monthly and weekly magazines. The readership of these magazines, it was felt, would respond to sophisticated advertising, and so Guinness started to use parodies of well-known poems. Among the authors whose work was rearranged were Lewis Carroll, Thomas Hood, Edward Lear, WS Gilbert, Chaucer, Longfellow, Wordsworth and Keats. There were several verses based on 'You are old, Father William', from *Alice in Wonderland*, of which one ran as follows:

> *'In my youth,' said his father, 'the Guinness I drank*
> *Kept me free from interior strife,*
> *And the fitness for which I've got Guinness to thank*
> *Has lasted the rest of my life.'*

When parodies of *Alice* were used by Guinness, there was a considerable increase in the sales of *Alice in Wonderland* and *Through the Looking Glass* – though how they affected Guinness sales is unknown!

Guinness also started to advertise in university magazines, and even went so far as to use verses in Latin to advertise the product to this educated audience. So popular were these that *The Times* published the verses and their accompanying animal drawings in 1936 – and someone wrote to Guinness looking for a translation. It was the first time that any product was advertised in Latin in an English newspaper.

But long before Guinness was paying for advertising, well-known authors were already doing it for them free of charge. In Dickens's sketch 'The Boarding House', a new resident comes to live in the boarding house. Mrs Bloss is a fat, red-faced lady, and her possessions arrive in instalments, the first of which consists of 'a large hamper of Guinness's Stout and an umbrella. Clearly Mrs Bloss is a lady with

excellent priorites.' Quite. And in *The Pickwick Papers* (1837), an illustration shows Sam and Tony Weller in the Blue Boar pub; in the background can be seen a card advertising 'Guinnes's Stout'. Mis-spelt, but unmistakably advertising.

On that very point of spelling, *The Comic English Grammar* ruled as follows in 1840:

> The Possessive case is distinguished by an apostrophe, with the letter 's' subjoined to it: as 'My soul's idol', 'A Pudding's end'... When the singular terminates in 'ss', the letter 's' is is sometimes dispensed with: as 'For Goodness' sake'. Nevertheless we have no objection to 'Guinness's Stout'.

Well, that's a relief! And isn't it interesting that as early as 1840 there is that happy conjunction of 'Guinness' and 'Goodness'.

In a *Punch* cartoon of 1884, Bismarck is shown at his desk, on which stand a tankard and a bottle labelled 'Guinness Extra Stout'. If you look closely, you can just make out a champagne bottle sitting expectantly beside the Guinness bottle, so presumably 'Bissy' was drinking black velvet – a drink invented in 1861 by a barman in a London pub who felt that champagne, being white, should go into mourning on the death of Prince Albert, and so mixed it with Guinness. This cartoon may account for the fact that a black velvet was at one time referred to as a 'Bismarck'.

It is claimed that no writer has made more literary allusions to Guinness than Joyce, but Guinness has generally confined its use of Joyce's references in its own advertising campaigns to Ireland, on the grounds that the average drinker outside Ireland would find them too enigmatic. What, for example, would foreigners make of the following characters from *Finnegans Wake*: Guinnghis Khan, Allfor Guineas, Ser Artur Ghinis, Mooseyeare Goorness? All the same, one Guinness ad in the UK featured an excerpt from *Finnegans Wake*, as follows: 'Foamous homely brew, bebattled by bottle, gageure de guegarre.' Try working that one out! But perhaps Joyce's most famous Guinnessism appears in *Ulysses*:

> Terence O'Ryan heard him and straight away brought him a crystal cup full of the foaming ebon ale which the noble twin brothers Bungiveagh and Bungardilaun brew ever in their divine alevat, cunning as the sons of deathless Leda. For they garner the succulent berries of the hop and mass and sift and bruise and brew them and they mix therewith sour juices and bring the must to the sacred fire and cease not night or day from their toil, those cunning brothers, lords of the vat.

Whether or not advertising actually helps to sell more Guinness — and the frustrating thing about advertising is that it's almost impossible, as Lord Leverhulme of Lever Bros famously lamented, to find out *which* 50% of the money spent on advertising is wasted — it is certainly true that no other alcoholic beverage has acquired the universal goodwill that Guinness has. Perhaps part of the reason for this is that Guinness has always abided by the principle that its advertising should be both excellent and in good taste. In any case, both Guinness advertising and Guinness sales have smiled through depressions, wars, recessions, fashions, changes in taste, economic and social changes and the coming of TV. Like the beer it helps to sell, Guinness advertising is good. It's in good taste and it reflects a product that is good, wholesome and well worth buying.

Promoting Guinness

Back in Dublin, I joined the happy band of 'town travellers', the team of four people plus their regional boss whose job it was to service the licensed trade in and around Dublin. In every way we were home again. We were back, so to speak, to the mother house. Back to that gorgeous smell of a new brew which Dubliners are so very familiar with. Back to the cobblestones, the shiny brasses, the well-painted walls and doors, the well-kept lavatories, the busy but friendly offices and staff and back to the St James's Gate people. The familiar faces. The chat. The Dublin and the Guinness sense of humour — and yes, there is such a thing as the Guinness sense of humour! As I settled back into life at Company HQ I began to branch out into new areas of work, starting with a new unit to deal with promotions.

Promotions

The Promotions Section of the Trade Department came into being in early 1964, although informally Guinness has been promoting its product since 1759. Ever since the very first brew, the cry went out from St James's Gate that Guinness was a unique and wonderful drink and worthy of purchase, and over the centuries it has been making this claim in a variety of ways, through advertising, through sponsorship of events like the Galway Oyster Festival and Punchestown Races. But the setting up of the Promotions Section established promotions as a separate entity rather

161

than a series of events looked after as part of the job of the various Trade Department regions and travellers.

One way or another I was very glad to be asked to accept the job of second-in-command of the new arrival. It had attractive ingredients – new, national, hard work and long hours, excitement, challenge, fun, people, imagination, creativity. It was made for me and, I felt, I for it.

There were five promotions managers, all male and all except one ex-travellers, and we had a back-up office team of four young women. It was an interesting little group, all of whom had to have several things in common such as liking and being good at handling people. We also had to be inventive by way of suggesting new promotions or new angles to existing promotions, flexible about working hours and prepared to work weekends when necessary, foxy in the sense of seeing through spurious applications for sponsorship, willing to at least consider virtually every application that came in to us, and social, gregarious and convivial. In fact we were a happy bunch who enjoyed our job and had some fun. It was probably the most agreeable group I ever worked with within the Company.

The work was divided partly by way of location and partly by way of type of event – sporting, cultural etc. We were the envy of many others at St James's Gate, as we were seen to be paid for enjoying ourselves by attending so many and such varied social events. Imagine being paid for doing that! Because of the nature of our jobs we also had a fairly good expenses allowance. In the hurly-burly of our work,

we were on duty for long hours, worked at week-ends, slept little, ate too much, sampled generously, put on weight, missed out on family life, were denied adequate exercise time, met countless people, read little and put up considerable mileage. In short, we had a great time and thoroughly enjoyed it all.

For me it meant several years of interesting work assessing, measuring and considering the spending of the Company's money on the promotion of our product – and the results of such operations. This is a difficult task, since there is no known way of accurately measuring the results of one's labours, no measuring tool, partly because we were dealing with attempts to measure such ill-defined items as 'goodwill', 'publicity', 'kudos', assets that are difficult to measure commercially. There is always an undertow of scepticism about one's motives for doing what one does – the suspicion that one is doing it for 'what's in it for me' – that tends to work against the desired outcome of good publicity, which makes assessing the benefits of work like this more difficult.

Like most Guinness travellers of that era I had been involved in several promotions in whatever region I was attached to, such as the greyhound racing in Cork, the oyster festival in Galway, the Moy festival in Ballina, Punchestown races in the Dublin region. But now I had left travelling behind, and all my attention was to be diverted to help organise and develop the whole concept of promotions at a national level. The rationale of promotions and sponsorship was straightforward. We wanted to show that Guinness, as a company, was prepared and happy to help and support both national and local ventures but with the proviso that, in deference to our stakeholders and shareholders, we expected something in return. The 'something' was that, as a result of our involvement, our name would be constantly before the public and that people would think well of us. That being so they would, we hoped, drink our product.

At the same time we took the view that there were many ways of being commercially efficient. And one of them was to help people and groups all over the country to organise and generate local or national events which would be good for their business and for their other interests. We offered advice, money, prizes, sponsorship of events. We were invited to sit on local committees. And we had *carte blanche* to organise anything we liked which we felt would get us desirable publicity and extra sales before, during and after the event. It was really using existing or invented social events for the benefit of all concerned. (Today it would merit some splendid term like 'business symbiosis'.)

When the news got around that we were setting up the new office the inevitable happened. It was translated into meaning that Guinness was open to all suggestions and to all applications for sponsorship. Requests flooded in. Anything from a black pudding eating championship to the Grand National – all was up for grabs. On one occasion we were actually requested to sponsor the funeral of a publican whose family thought it would be a proper thing for Guinness to do and guaranteeing us that only Guinness would be served at the wake!

It took a few months for the dust to settle and the first thing we had to do was set out a routine for examining all requests which came into us. That meant listing a few basic criteria against which to do an assessment and we used that as a kind of benchmark to guide us about our next move. We had to turn down far more requests than we could meet, and rejections usually resulted in a sour taste in the rejected camp. That did us no good. But what could we do? Abolish the whole idea of promotions? Spend countless millions on them? Spread the budget so thinly that nothing was worthy of publicity and there was therefore little or nothing in it for us? Or press on as best we could, spend our budget, and see what happens? That is what we did.

Our next move was to divide promotions into two groups – local and national. Both were important but required different handling. A local promotion might consist of something like a pub darts competition which would run for weeks and generate a lot of pint drinking in the process. It might easily merit some local press coverage and prizes could range from a modest cash prize to a first-class darts set.

National events such as Punchestown Races or the Galway Oyster Festival were on a different scale. Publicity was via all media and was in action before, during and after the event. We used such events as opportunities to invite people, Irish and overseas, to come as our guests and enjoy a day out. They were excellent opportunities for us to act as hosts. After all, we were in the leisure business and it was appropriate for us to use leisure opportunities to do what leisure should do – have fun! In acting as hosts, Guinness personnel were expected and very happy to join in the fun, while at the same time making sure that the event was going smoothly. We tried always to have things well organised – but not so organised or regimented that it interfered with enjoyment. We also tried to have a fall-back or support plan in case something went wrong. Like all jobs, this had its problems because it was not easy always to be strictly controlled about having a sociable drink or two with our invited guests while they were 'out for the day' and thoroughly enjoying themselves – uninhibited. For us it was mixing business with pleasure.

We got involved in festivals and fetes, drama and greyhound racing, the Festival of Kerry, Puck Fair in Killorglin, the Listowel Wren Boys, Kilkenny Beer Festival, the Castlebar Song Contest, Enniscorthy Fleadh Ceoil, Moy Salmon Festival, Enniscorthy Strawberry Fair, Killybegs Angling Competition, Sculling on the Liffey, Comhaltas Ceoltóirí Éireann – you name it and Guinness may well have been involved in it.

The Wexford Festival rescue operation

Way back in the 1960s, when Lord Boyd was MD of our parent company, he frequently and regularly came to St

CATHAL GANNON

Come with me now for a few minutes and I'll show you something which I think you'd like to see. It is one of the last things you would ever expect to find in a brewery.

It's a secret workshop with one man in it. His name is Cathal Gannon. What does he do in there? He makes harpsichords! It's true. And he draws his normal weekly wages as a carpenter in Guinness for doing it. Not only does Cathal make harpsichords, but he has a vast interest in, and knowledge of, old clocks, antiques and old Dublin.

Cathal has been interested for many years in ancient keyboard instruments. Years ago, he made a clavichord (an instrument that is the forerunner of today's piano), a percussive instrument of almost gossamer delicacy. Next he restored an 1805 Clementi 'square' piano. Then he made a quilled keyboard instrument of the kind referred to as a pair of virginals. (It is believed that it got its name because it was used in convents in the sixteenth and early seventeenth centuries to lead the virginals or hymns to the Virgin.)

Then came the harpsichords. He has made several of them and they all required a most demanding degree of skill, patience and most delicate handling.

Some of the Gannon harpsichords have been played by the world's leading players and at venues which include a performance of Bach's St Matthew Passion by the Guinness Choir, the Virtuosi di Roma at the Dublin Music Festival in 1959, the Goethe Institut in Dublin, in the Pillar Room in the Rotunda Hospital in Dublin and at many broadcasts by RTÉ. For reasons that I do not pretend to understand, I was intrigued to know from Cathal that, in the making of the plucking mechanisms of his harpsichords, pigs' bristles are used.

Cathal Gannon has left his mark on Irish musical history and for that was conferred with an Honorary Degree of Master of Arts by Trinity College in 1978, a very well-deserved accolade!

Cathal Gannon passed away in May 1999.

James's Gate to keep an eye on things in Ireland and when he was 'in residence' he usually generated a buzz of excitement and activity. He was a big man in every way — tall, expansive, shrewd, positive.

Early one morning, my phone rang and Boyd asked me to come and see him in his office. After a genial exchange of pleasantries he showed me a piece in *The Irish Times* about the critical condition of the Wexford Opera Festival which, according to the article, was about to be wound up because it was broke. He gave me three days to investigate the whole matter of the festival thoroughly and give him my report and recommendations about a possible Guinness rescue operation by way of sponsorship. It was a dream brief for anyone in promotions. I was off!

In brief, my investigation included tapping into anybody who was anybody in the musical scene in Ireland. It required cold, hard financial facts. I also had to assess the cultural and commercial value to Ireland of keeping Wexford alive. It had become one of our cultural gems and had acquired international fame in the world of music and the arts, even on a very restricted budget. It was a living example of the contribution made by Ireland to music.

In any civilised country the arts should have an important place in the lives of its people, and besides, a festival like Wexford helps to build up the international image of Ireland and its cultural heritage, one result of which is that it brings visitors to our shores who spend money here, including money spent on Guinness. Guinness cannot measure the amount spent, but common sense tells us that sales are increased by tourists so what's good for Ireland's tourist trade is good for Guinness.

My researches included dreaming up types of sponsorships and assessing what would be the likely benefits and costs of sponsoring the Wexford Opera Festival to Guinness. It took three days — and the best part of three nights. My report and recommendation went to Boyd. Within the hour I was back in his office, where we discussed the whole matter. He accepted the report and signed it as approval to go ahead and put all my recommendations into effect. Wexford was saved, and it is still going strong. If Guinness had not come to the rescue, someone else might have done so, but we had got there first and we've always been glad about that.

The Guinness Radio Club

People working in a company can reflect the image of their company in all kinds of ways and, in the case of Guinness, most of what is projected is for the benefit of the company. As part of the Company's projection of its 'with it' image the Company had a radio programme on Radio Telefís Éireann called *The Guinness Radio Club*. The Company sponsored it and, as part of my job in the Promotions Section, I had the job of producing and presenting it. It was a half-hour, weekly, late-night miscellany programme. While we had to abide by certain station rules about blatant advertising we were (among other things) able to mention whatever promotions activities we happened to be involved in at any time.

For instance, when we sponsored the Wexford Festival of Opera we interviewed Wexford people on the air about the upcoming or current programme and we'd bring in some facts about what the festival meant to Wexford by way of increase in spending in the town during the festival and what the Guinness input meant. When we sponsored the Galway Oyster Festival we did a whole programme about oysters and food and Guinness. When the Guinness Choir or the Guinness Players were competing at music or drama festivals the radio programme dealt with the festivals and the extent of the Guinness involvement. When we wanted to boost sales in the Cork region we went down to Cork and devoted a programme to the history and involvement of Guinness in Cork. That particular programme was broadcast from the RTÉ Cork studios.

All of this was aimed at what might be described as the 'soft sell' of Guinness because we were projecting an image of the Company as being involved in virtually all aspects of life in Ireland. Any 'over-sell' might easily have generated an undesirable reaction from listeners so we had to be careful as to how to package the programme so that it remained interesting and entertaining without overdoing things. That's one reason why we kept one of the most popular items on it – horse racing tips for forthcoming race meetings whether or not we were sponsoring any of the races.

Wherever possible, we used the talents of Guinness personnel to cover such areas as gardening hints, book reviews, theatre and cinema reviews. All in all we built up quite an audience during the years we were on air and we dealt with an enthusiastic post bag from various parts of the country plus a few from listeners in the UK.

Another desirable spin-off from the programme was that our reps around the country had an interesting topic to talk about when they called to our customers. Invariably the

THE GUINNESS CHOIR

On 16 May 1951, the Guinness Choir gave its inaugural performance (in a double bill with the Guinness Players) with Gilbert and Sullivan's Trial by Jury in the Rupert Guinness Hall right in the heart of the Guinness Brewery, with all parts played by Guinness people.

The choir's founder and conductor was Victor Leeson, an indefatigable man who has, virtually single-handed, maintained such enthusiasm and drive among the choir members that it has been possible to take them through a most extensive repertoire which includes works by Bach, Handel, Haydn, Rossini, Berlioz, Balfe, Stanford and Britten. The choir is modestly proud of major awards won at several international choral competitions.

The Guinness Choir has been one of the finest achievements of Guinness personnel in any of their extra-mural activities. It brought together men and women of all ranks and grades in the Company who had music as a common bond. It was one of the first groups within the Company to start quietly dismantling the old barriers between layers of personnel in the sheer joy of singing.

An unplanned result of the Choir's great success is that it couldn't help achieving some highly valuable publicity for the Company. Thankfully, it thrives to this day.

locals had heard some item which was of particular interest to them and that led to discussion and chat – good for pubbery! In fact we had several requests from our customers asking to be allowed on the programme to talk about this or that item of local interest.

So the Guinness image was kept constantly in the minds of a wide range of people. There is no way of knowing for sure if it had any effect on sales, but it is reasonable to assume that it played some part in the desirable projection of the Company and its product. Alas, when the long arm of the necessary 'cutbacks' came to the whole Company, the radio programme was one of its victims and we came off air.

The Guinness Radio Club was a 'first' in the history of Guinness and in the history of brewing – at least in Ireland. Another example of the Company's innovative policies.

My radio and TV career

As it happened I didn't in fact come off air. Like four of the five Byrne siblings I was involved in broadcasting from a very early age. I first went on the radio at the age of eight as a member of our school choir singing Christmas carols and I've never quite come off air since. In the period 1938–78 I was very much involved in both radio and TV broadcasting.

Because I was working with Guinness, I was not a full-time broadcaster but I managed to clock up a lot of airtime as an absorbing hobby. I wrote and presented radio talks. I wrote short stories which were read by members of the

RTÉ Rep Company. On a weekly radio programme, I interviewed various people, famous or otherwise, Irish or visiting Ireland, who were in the news for some reason or another. I presented morning programmes as a disc jockey. I wrote and presented several series of programmes which were a mixture of music and a story, for example a series on the well-known ballets. And I did some live commentaries on special occasions, such as the visit of the Pope to Ireland.

When RTÉ television went on air on 31 December 1961 it had a profound effect on Ireland and on the Irish. The whole country was watching it. My first appearance on television was five nights after opening night, when I interviewed someone on a current affairs programme. After that came many years of TV work, and with it a certain amount of public recognition for me as a broadcaster, which in turn reflected on the company I worked for, as it became known that I also worked for Guinness. The Company took the view that it was a positive asset to have a TV 'personality' on its staff – in a Company like Guinness with its nationwide business interests, it helps the overall image of the Company if they have people in public life who are seen to be playing their part in the country's activities.

Come to think of it, though, there were one or two people who were not quite happy about it. Occasionally when a Guinness traveller was out on the road on business matters we had with us one of our bosses who, quite rightly, wanted to keep directly in touch with our business and also to keep an eye on the way their staff was behaving. During the first few years of Irish television, when it was still a novelty, the whole country was tuned in and every programme was analysed out of its mind. The presenters became household names, almost household possessions. One result was that, when I visited someone on business and my boss happened to be with me, they virtually ignored the poor man completely and spent the time talking to me about television. In the end, the boss simply left me to my own devices, which suited all concerned.

After more than four years in Promotions, I was asked, in 1968, to set up yet another new unit within Guinness Group Sales (Ireland) Ltd, and that's the next part of this story.

Training publicans

If you were to stop and ask any decent pint drinker in Ireland the question 'What's a pub for?' he'd probably think you were having him on, or else that you were some harmless half-wit. Yet this was the question which was posed to the audience at the opening session of their nine-day course in licensed house management. We were all amazed at some of the answers.

At that time there was a wholly-owned subsidiary of the Guinness Group called Murtagh Properties Ltd, which had been set up to buy and run a number of pubs in the Republic of Ireland. In 1968 they owned ten pubs in various parts of the country and they found that they were frequently receiving requests from some other publicans in their area as to what system Murtagh Properties used for stock control. To retain the goodwill of their neighbours (who were, after all, customers of ours) they did their best to cope with these requests for advice. Then someone suggested that Guinness should organise lectures on the subject. That led to a suggestion that Guinness should run a series of one-day courses in stock control. We had to call a halt there and think about the whole matter.

Since the introduction of Guinness trade inspectors in the late 1890s it was realised that, whatever about the quality of the stout as it left the Brewery, there was little or no permanent control over its quality and appearance as served to the consumer. In fact it was this loss of control over quality, with its concomitant adulteration of Guinness stout by a few publicans and then complaints from consumers, that was the reason inspectors were introduced in the first place. In other words it was not enough that we should produce, market and sell our goods. We should be able to follow them up to the point where they are presented to the consumer. But how to do that?

We obviously could not act as policemen always on the beat to catch out culprits. Yet we had to protect the interests of the consumers on whom we depended for our existence. We decided that bar staff should be trained how to do their job well, and since no such training was then available, we should grab the initiative and set up training courses.

We decided to begin by training licensed house owners (or their sons or daughters who were in the trade with them), managers and charge-hands. These were the people who were dealing directly with the consumers. They were also the people who were managing and controlling licensed premises throughout Ireland. A decision was taken to set up the Guinness Licensed House Management Course, and I was made director-in-charge of this original and exciting project and asked to open for business three months later. (I always though that that title 'director' was given in order to make the course itself, not me, sound important. But still, it was the first time I was allowed to use it.)

Each course had twenty-five participants, male and female, from all over Ireland. The course was free, but students had to pay for their accommodation in Dublin and for their travel expenses. Each course ran for nine full days and included visits to Murtagh Property pubs and others in the evenings. We had a farewell supper at St James's Gate, when framed diplomas were presented to those who had satisfactorily completed the course. They took this home with them and hung it in their bar for all their customers to see. They were also given a specially designed tie or scarf, which it was the exclusive right of the graduate to wear.

At our first session we invited a panel of well-known Irish personalities to come and discuss the question of what a pub is for. What makes a good pub? What do people want most in a pub? What do women like most about a pub? What's wrong with our licensing hours? We video-recorded this session and used it as an opener for all of the courses. The point we were trying to make was that we are all so busy with the day-to-day details of our job that few of us take the time to stand back and ask ourselves what it is all about.

In our first term (Oct/Nov) we had 200 students. In our second term (Jan/Mar) we had 425. And so it grew. Some lecturers (insurance employees, policemen, fire-brigade workers) came from outside the Company and, where appropriate, were paid a fee. Others came from inside the Guinness organisation (Murtagh Properties house managers, accountants, a chef, tax experts, draught/bottled Guinness experts and so on) and were happy to contribute as part of their job.

Looking back on it, the whole concept of a brewery offering free training for bar staff was highly original and well worth while. It helped members of the licensed trade to increase or at least maintain sales and profits. It helped relations between Guinness and the licensed trade. It helped outside interests like the police to get their message across. It helped Guinness to sustain the quality of their products as served to consumers and that helped our sales and profits. And, most important of all, it helped the people who kept Guinness and the licensed outlets in business – the consumers – to have what they wanted and what they paid for.

Once the course was up and running smoothly, the inevitable happened – I got bored. The excitement of a new challenge faded. Fortunately I was able to hand it over to a colleague and I was off to Corporate Planning.

Continued on page 187

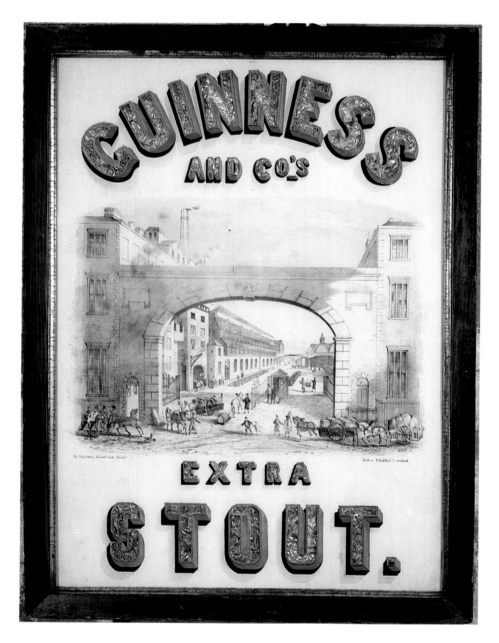

One of the very earliest pieces of showcard advertising for display in Irish pubs

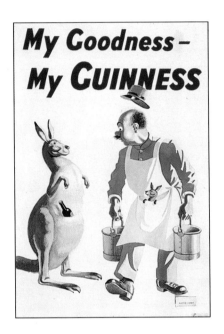

When Guinness gave its advertising account to the London firm of SH Benson in 1928, it could not have foreseen the incredible impact that Guinness advertising was to have on the general public. Most of this was due to one man — an artist called John Gilroy. His inspired Guinness animals captured and kept for decades the interest of millions of people in Guinness.

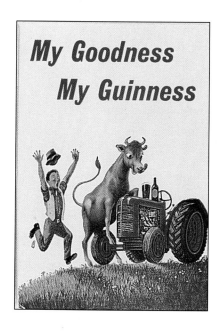

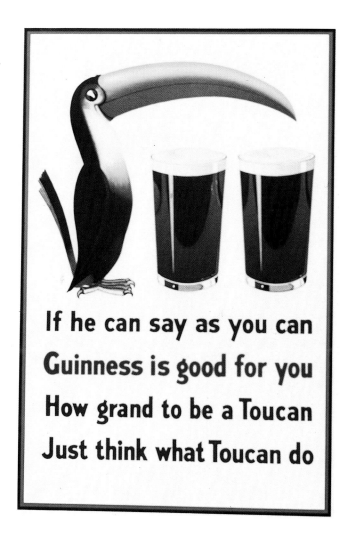

It was the punny little verse on this poster that became famous.

Another of John Gilroy's masterpieces. Thousands of letters came into the Company saying that the glass in the ostrich's neck was the wrong way up!

One of the most famous of all Guinness ads. Oddly enough, when the artist Gilroy produced his first drawing of this his son pointed out that the angle of the girder would make it impossssible to balance it on the man's head. So Gilroy corrected the error and never looked back!

MILLION
GUINNESS
for strength every day

Drawing by J. Gilroy

G.E. 1246

As the New Gnu knew very soon at the Zoo Guinness is good for you

SOMETIMES WE FEEL
THE WHOLE WORLD
IS AGUINNESS

It is. So it isn't.

Take up Irish history tonight

GUINNESS

Familiarity breeds content.

The dark fantastic.

A James's 'gape' at
Guinness and Dublin

A Guinness Museum
exhibition
at the Visitors' Centre

Mon - Fri 9.30 - 4.30

February to August 1982

1882 - 1941

Black is beautiful

One of our great natural resources

A selection of old beer bottles and a tankard. They are on view in the Guinness Museum.

*Tools of the
cooper's craft*

Continued from page 170

Corporate Planning

Beaver and diversification

A man called Sir Hugh Beaver, a consultant engineer, was one of a team of contractors employed by Guinness to build its brewery at Park Royal in London in the early 1930s. Beaver master-minded the project. It was highly successful and Guinness were very impressed at the way Beaver performed. So much so that, when the job of managing director of Arthur Guinness Son and Co. Ltd became vacant ten years later, Beaver was offered and took on the job. He proved to be a brilliant MD. Brought in from the outside he was not saddled with Guinness traditions or practices and this allowed the aptly named new MD to look objectively and dispassionately at the Company, its effectiveness, its product, its place in the world of business and commerce, its people, and its future. No panic. Sales and profits were fine. All was well. But a review was indicated. And what follows is a simplified account of that review and what happened as a result of it.

One of the things Beaver started looking at was the beer market in general and in the UK and Ireland in particular and the place of Guinness in that market. His research into the comparative performance of other brewers in other markets threw up some interesting facts. For instance, in the German beer market in the early 1900s the situation was that, of all beers consumed there, 85% was dark beer and 15% was light beer. But, and this was a crucial point, by the early 1950s the position was precisely reversed showing that dark beers then held 15% of the market with light beers holding 85%. For Beaver, that posed the question, What would be the result if such a thing were to happen in the UK and Irish beer markets? He was rightly somewhat troubled by the idea that we had 'all our eggs in one basket'.

As far as the UK market was concerned, there was no point in Guinness producing light beers because no tied-house licensee would agree to sell them in competition with his existing light beers. Selling Guinness stout was OK because it merely added to the list of beers available in his pub. But another ale in competition with his own – no. So, if not light beers in the UK, why not try somewhere else? What about the US? After all, imported Guinness stout had been on sale in the US for a long time and perhaps with the Guinness name and fame behind it and 'free' houses in which to sell it, Guinness could combine brewing ale with brewing stout in, say, New York?

It was tried, but it failed. There were several reasons for that. One was the fortune it would have cost to advertise and promote the product. Another was the entrenched position taken and defended by the American brewers since the end of prohibition in 1933, which amounted to a shut-out of non-American brewers. That put Beaver off attempting to brew light beers overseas, at least temporarily. So what about diversification into non-brewing activities?

Apart from the great success of *The Guinness Book of Records*, of which more anon, came other interests, such as buying the UK confectionery company William Nuttall;

BY-PRODUCTS

Lest anyone should think that the Guinness Brewery in Dublin has only one marketable product, it is worth while reminding ourselves that the Company has other items on their menu. These are very minor activities compared with brewing, but they were always profit-making, job-creating and useful products for the marketplace.

Spent grains was one such by-product of brewing. When the sparging has finished, and the malt has been made almost dry of its liquids, it leaves behind in the brewing vessel (called a kieve) a thick deposit of damp material for all the world like a giant plate of fairly hot porridge. At that point three men, stripped to the waist and wearing large clog-type boots, got into the kieve. Using large shovels they moved these 'spent' grains into an aperture in the centre of the kieve floor where the grains fell down into wagons waiting on the narrow-gauge railway below. Men doing this work had to be very healthy and fit and, because of the nature of this hot and steamy work, they got an extra allowance of porter during their shift so that dehydration was avoided.

The full wagons went off to a loading point where the spent grains were put into lorries owned mostly by farmers who were happy to pay for this valuable animal feed. They were mostly owners of dairy herds in the Dublin region, but pig-owners were also glad to buy these grains. In all, the Company was selling over 70,000 tons of spent grains per annum.

The Company also did a good business in selling spent hops. These were recovered from brewing vessels called 'hop backs' in the same way as spent grains from the kieves and, at that point, one of two things could happen to the spent hops. About 70% of them were taken off to a hop-drying plant where, after drying, they were filled into sacks and dispatched to fertiliser manufacturers in Ireland and in the UK, where they became a very useful source of humus – the substance resulting from the slow decomposition of organic matter and a valuable constituent of soil. The remaining 30% were left undried and removed by local farmers and used partly as fertiliser and partly as animal/poultry feed.

Yeast is another of the Company's by-products. When you put yeast into the brewing chain it feeds on the sugars which were extracted from the malt but it consumes so much that, in every brew, it multiplies itself ten times over. The result is a very considerable surplus of yeast over and above what is required for use in the next brew. What to do with an annual surplus of 4000 tons of it? Several things.

Some of it is made into autolysed yeast and sold to a UK firm who use it in the production of gravies, soups etc. Some is sold to various distilleries who do not propagate their own yeasts and therefore have to buy some. Some is used to produce Guinness Yeast Extract – or GYE as it was called. This was a product on sale in Ireland but had only a very limited market. It was used as a type of Bovril and also in the flavouring of gravies, soups etc. Some is sold to farmers as dried yeast and used in the production of animal feed in Ireland, the UK and various countries in Europe.

Lastly, a by-product of brewing is the production of carbon dioxide gas. During fermentation, for every 300 pints of stout produced, about 8lb of carbon dioxide is produced as a by-product. This is collected, purified by chemical means, and compressed into a liquid. Several hundred tons of this is produced every year and it is sold to beer bottlers and mineral water manufacturers in Ireland.

becoming involved in the pharmaceutical business by establishing Twyford Laboratories Ltd; and by buying the pharmaceutical company Crooks. There were other diversifications but, in *toto*, things did not work out well. Some did OK – especially in the short term. Some were a failure and were sold off later on at a considerable loss. The whole exercise pointed to the conclusion that, as a brewing company, Guinness did its job very successfully, but once it went off into the pond of diversifications unrelated to brewing they found themselves unequal to the task of dealing with the commercialised piranha fish and they withdrew bloodied if not bowed. At least that's what happened in the UK. But what about the situation in Ireland?

In Ireland, Guinness had almost 90% of the total beer market and that meant that it was very difficult indeed to achieve any worthwhile growth in sales or profits. But there were definite signs of the international growth of sales in ales and lagers. Furthermore, unlike in the UK, most licensed premises in Ireland were 'free' houses so they could sell whatever they liked. Lastly there was a Canadian brewer nosing his way around parts of Ireland – and not as a tourist. Things pointed to Guinness becoming involved in ale brewing and Beaver decided to purchase at least some of the small ale breweries in various parts of the country and also to consider brewing a lager.

The deal was on and a new company was set up which was 66% owned by Guinness and 33% owned by the large English brewers, Ind Coope. Within a short time, this new company gobbled up the Irish ale breweries including Cherry's, Macardle Moore, Smithwicks, Perry's and Cairns. By 1958, two years before he retired as MD, Beaver had bought at least 66% of all ale breweries in Ireland. In 1959, with one year still to go in his Guinness career, the Guinness-owned Harp lager brewery in Dundalk produced a brew of Harp lager for the first time. Apart from anything else it did, these acquisitions safeguarded Guinness brewing operations in Ireland by being well prepared for any real or predicted sustained and substantial swing to light beers. They had covered their back.

Diversification in Ireland did not end there, because Beaver had sown the seeds of exciting non-brewing diversification. In the late 1960s, Guinness in Dublin decided to have a look at some possibilities and started things by setting up a small unit (two males, one female secretary) and calling it 'Corporate Planning'. For a period of two years of its existence I was one of those males.

The Emerald Star Line

The approach was logical. Since beer-drinking is a leisure occupation it was sensible for Guinness to have a look at the leisure scene in Ireland. It seemed reasonable also to look in particular at parts of the country which had not gained as much as they should have from the general growth of prosperity in the late 1960s. Putting such thoughts together, and following a suggestion from a Guinness staff man, the first non-brewing diversification project to be taken on by Guinness in Ireland was an investment in cabin cruisers on the River Shannon. Booking started at Easter 1970 and the initial investment, including a Bord Fáilte grant, was £600,000 (about £4.5m in today's money).

It started with twenty-three cruisers and the plan was

to bring that up to a hundred. It was also mooted that, if all went well with the boat-hire end of things, Guinness might consider going into the boat-building business and indeed into the ordered development of the Shannon, areas such as the building of small riverbank restaurants and provision stores.

The boat-hire business has been a success — both directly and indirectly. Flying under the flag of Emerald Star Line (ESL) business has gone from strength to strength. Some forty-five people are now employed full-time between Shannon and the main booking office in Dublin. In the Shannon area itself ESL and its boats have brought countless thousands of Irish and overseas visitors, and that has resulted in the spending of millions of pounds locally and has therefore met the hopes and expectations of the early planners. It is an example of successful corporate planning.

The Guinness Book of Records

On 10 November 1951, Sir Hugh Beaver, the managing director of Guinness, was out with a shooting party on the famous North Slob by the River Slaney in County Wexford, tucked away in the south-east corner of Ireland, when some golden plover flew overhead. Beaver fired and missed. That evening, while having a pint or two, someone suggested to Beaver that the reason he missed was because golden plover was the fastest of all birds. This statement was instantly challenged by another member of the party who named some other bird as the fastest. There was a bit of an argument about which was the fastest bird and a lot more pint-drinking before the night was out.

Back in his office in London, Beaver talked to his staff member Christopher Chataway (one of the two men who set the pace for Roger Bannister in May 1964, when Bannister became the first man ever to run a mile in less than four minutes). This conversation led to Beaver and Chataway inviting the twins Norris and Ross McWhirter, who were running a fact-finding agency in London, to lunch. And that lunch led eventually to the launch in August 1955 of *The Guinness Book of Records*.

The argument in the pub about the golden plover that Beaver had failed to shoot led him to realise that there must be countless questions debated nightly in the 85,000 or so pubs in Britain and Ireland but with no definitive reference book available to settle the arguments about records. From there, take into account pubs and drinking establishments all over the world and you would surely have a world bestseller.

Beaver was right. Within a few months of its first appearance in 1955 *The Guinness Book of Records* became No. 1 on the bestseller list, with total sales of 51,969. By 1956 total sales had passed 5 million copies. The first non-English (French) edition appeared in 1962. By 1998 it was being published in 17 non-English languages including Danish, Dutch, Finnish, Italian, Norwegian, Portugese, Spanish, Swedish, Czech, Greek, Hungarian, Polish,

German, Japanese. In 1974, the book became the top-selling copyright book in the history of publishing with total sales of 23.9 million copies. *The Guinness Book of Records* had earned the right to be included itself in *The Guinness Book of Records!*

The making and selling of *The Guinness Book of Records* became a very important profit-making diversification for the Guinness Company. That was good for all of us who worked there and for shareholders. And it showed that some diversifications can and do work very well – even in Guinness.

The *Book* is a source of endless interest and entertainment, and that made it a very acceptable gift from Guinness to people to whom we wanted to say thank you for helping us out in some small way, as an impromptu birthday present or as a hand-out at a Guinness press conference to announce a sports sponsorship or whatever. With its Guinness name and its Guinness connection it was a constant reminder of the Company, its product, and its involvement in matters of topical and worthwhile interest at home and abroad. It was good PR.

As Guinness travellers all over the country, the *Book* was a frequent source of chat between us and our customers. Discussion of its contents was a shoehorn into convivial conversation and that often eased us into business matters and resulted in business well done and good trade relationships established and maintained.

The *Book* has achieved a unique, concrete and clear-cut

GWEF

The Guinness Workers' Employment Fund Ltd – known simply as GWEF, started in the 1960s, when a few of the employees began to wonder how they could help stem the depressing and increasing tide of emigration from Ireland at that time. They decided that one answer was to create jobs at home, and for their inspiration they went back to Benjamin Franklin and his maxim 'for want of a nail the shoe was lost' etc. They reasoned that it is not just carelessness which causes the loss – one must first purchase the nail, but the snag is that the price of it may not be available. How often has a good idea had to be abandoned for lack of capital?

And so they set up GWEF, which was a fund into which all employees of all ranks were invited to contribute a shilling a week. Over a thousand employees signed up, and within its first seven years GWEF had paid out some £23,000 in loans. Money keeps coming in and loans keep going out. GWEF is operated by a committee, which examines each application for a loan. It studies each project and interviews the applicants. Sometimes the Company itself becomes involved by way of granting loans on a fifty-fifty basis – in other words, half of the loan comes from the Company and half from GWEF.

The scheme is not confined to projects in Dublin.

To date, projects in over twelve counties have received loans as cash injections to help them to get started or to continue or expand an existing enterprise. The projects include furniture-making, souvenir design and making, stained glass manufacture, knitting, building, pottery, jewellery, agricultural operations, co-operative societies, weaving, printing, boat-building. In the early 1960s, for example, the potential of the River Shannon as a holiday amenity began to show great possibilities. The purchase and building of holiday cruisers was up and running. GWEF and Guinness combined paid out loans amounting to £9000 to help get this whole project under way and today cruising on the Shannon is responsible for hundreds of jobs on Shannonside and millions of pounds spent in Ireland by cruising visitors.

Apart from anything else it has done, GWEF stands as yet another example of how the Guinness Company and its people are intimately woven into the intricate pattern of life in Ireland to an extent and in ways which are virtually impossible to enumerate or evaluate. The big 'G' is ubiquitous. What's good for Ireland is good for Guinness, is the thinking.

as published. They employ a team of research people throughout the world who apply a very complex series of criteria which have to be met before an item is accepted for the *Book*. Every post brings in a host of wacky suggestions and claims by people who think they have achieved an item fit for inclusion.

Most claims are made about ladder climbing, longest paper chain, longest paper clip chain, human centipede, darts, line dancing and that sort of thing. Acceptance of any record claim demands incontrovertible evidence that a record has been accomplished. And this evidence has to be such that it satisfies the *Book's* team of researchers and also be such that it is able to resolve any possible challenge in the future by subsequent competitors.

It is widely accepted that the inclusion of the word 'Guinness' in the title of this book was the major factor in the successful launching of it on the world. After that, it secured its success by its contents. It is also widely accepted that, because of the world-wide appeal of the Book (with its concomitant high market awareness factor – 88% in the UK), it has contributed substantially to awareness of a beer called Guinness which, logically, must result in developing desired sales and profits. Surely the classic example of mutualism.

Other flurries outside St James's Gate

One of the main aims of corporate planning is to avoid the mistake of making wrong investments. So the Company

authority. It is the 'last word' – the definite reference point. So it is not surprising that the publishers go to extraordinary lengths in order to ensure and verify the facts examined various ideas (many of them submitted by Guinness personnel at St James's Gate who saw the dawning of something worth while) and spent a lot of time and money investigating possibilities. Some of them were not connected with the leisure business but nonetheless they were examined and assessed and (mostly) turned down. That was a bit depressing for the corporate planners but it had the sound, if unexciting, compensation that unwise investments were avoided.

Meantime the Company became involved in the production and marketing of mushrooms. It got into the preparation and selling of meats. Almost inevitably it made at least one mistake by becoming involved in a failed joint venture with an overseas company setting up a manufacturing company in Ireland.

Apart from the Emerald Star Line, most of these diversifications petered out for one reason or another, at least partly because the Company had tried to manage them by using Guinness personnel, who were not trained in the management of anything other than the production and selling of high-quality beers. Dipping their toes into unfamiliar waters proved, on the whole, to be unsuccessful. In truth, it is doubtful if Guinness actually lost money in these flurries outside St James's Gate but likewise it is doubtful if they made a profit out of them either. And the lessons learned must have been at least partly applicable to the general management of the Company's extended Irish brewing operations plus internal problems which were on the horizon. They were going to need that extra experience in the not-too-distant future.

Corporate planning was a job which required a strong input of creativity, imagination, practicality, and the ability to put a strong case in favour of, or against, proposals. It also needed the crucial input of sound financial experts with the particular ability of putting cold figures on any proposition so that the correct information was available prior to decision taking. An interesting and exciting experience in business matters.

Training

During my years at St James's Gate, it always struck me as passing strange that directors of the Company (with at least one exception) did not have extensive training as company directors. They might have been, for instance, a brewer or an engineer or an accountant, in which cases they were obviously trained in their particular speciality, but there was little or no actual training in how to be an effective Board member. What I have in mind here would be a full-time intensive at least one-year course abroad, where participants would mix with the next set of world business leaders. Somehow or other, the reasoning seemed to be that if you were a good brewer or chemist or accountant then the chances were that you would make a good and effective director. Quite an assumption, as subsequent events were to demonstrate.

But if you were a good tradesman or a good sales representative, then the theory and practice were that you needed some extra training to fit you for a job to which you were about to be promoted. In addition, all non-Board members were expected to attend courses in the latest techniques to hit their own particular sphere of operations in the Company – computers, electronics, materials handling, salesmanship etc. This made sense and the results of this training usually more than justified the cost of it.

It is not irrelevant to make these comments because it showed yet again the attitude of Guinness management towards the rest of personnel. It obviously believed that while the troops needed training (which indeed they did) the top officers did not. This attitude had been handed down right from the first Arthur Guinness to the third Lord Iveagh – a span of six chairmen who, somehow or other, had learned how to be successful businessmen without any training in management – other than watching how their predecessors did it. And for almost two centuries, the system worked well – before running into very serious trouble.

When I finished my innings with Corporate Planning, my next job was in Training. I was not particularly keen on this move but, as things turned out, I was very glad it happened.

The Training Department

The Training Department was given a satisfactory annual budget with which to do its job – which was to provide whatever training was necessary to enable personnel to do their job effectively – plus staff plus a well-furnished and well-equipped training centre. When I arrived there, the total staff amounted to some eight people.

To find out what training to provide was a two-pronged procedure. Training officers visited all departments and discussed with each departmental head what his department's training requirements were for the coming 'academic year'. The second prong was that training officers themselves would propose training subjects which they considered suitable for personnel. Some of this training was technical and carried out on the site where the work was done; some of it, in the form of lectures for example, was

THE IVEAGH TRUST

Over the last two to three centuries Dublin was unique in the high proportion of its population living in squalid tenements. At the beginning of the twentieth century, more than half of the families in the city lived in these tenements and one-third of the entire population of Dublin lived in one-roomed tenements – the bulk of them overcrowded and highly insanitary. In fact Dublin in those days had the reputation of being the unhealthiest, worst-housed city in the British Isles and the resultant extremely high mortality and disease rates were a central concern in all discussions of public health and housing reform. Working conditions, diet, leisure activities, unhygienic habits and fertility rates all played their parts in this appalling situation.

In 1890, when Sir Edward Cecil Guinness was Chairman of the Guinness Company, he founded a philanthropic organisation and called it the Guinness Trust. It was set up with the declared objective of 'providing housing and related amenities for the labouring poor in London and in Dublin'. Its initial endowment amounted to £200,000 for work in London plus £50,000 for work in Dublin, which makes a total of about £18m in today's money.

In 1903, the Dublin part of the fund plus its London-based administration were separated from the combined fund and thereafter was managed from its Dublin HQ. It also changed its name to the Iveagh Trust, following Edward Cecil's elevation to the peerage.

The trust now has over 800 dwellings and 130 hostel beds in Dublin. It is the largest voluntary housing body in Ireland. Iveagh Trust dwellings are located in five areas of the city but perhaps the best-known are the monumental blocks of flats and other buildings erected between 1893 and 1915 at Bull Alley and Kevin Street near St Patrick's Cathedral.

Two popular misconceptions might be righted here. The Guinness Brewery and the Iveagh Trust are now two quite separate organisations and there is no financial connection between them. Furthermore, the function of the Iveagh Trust is not to provide accommodation for Brewery personnel or for any sectional interests. It is to provide housing for working-class people in general.

The Iveagh Trust is one of Ireland's major philanthropic institutions, the oldest and much the largest non-governmental housing body in Ireland today.

done in the training centre; and some of it was done outside the Company premises, perhaps even abroad.

Under the general heading of 'training' the department was responsible for the education grants given to boys and lads. One of my first jobs was to dismantle the existing system of administering it and bring it up to date with a new system. In the 1960s the Dickensian system was as near as dammit to male clerks with starched collars and whiskers sitting on high stools at even higher desks and, complete with quill pens, daily entering attendance figures of boys and lads at technical schools. Ploughing through vast and dusty ledgers was not exactly mind-challenging, but we cleared up an antediluvian system and all was simple and easy to operate after that.

The department was also responsible for managing what was called the 'outward-bound' schools. These operated in the UK and, every year, the Company selected eight boys (or lads) usually on the grounds of general character, and paid all expenses for them to attend a mountain school at Eskdale in the Lake District in England or the Outward Bound Sea School at Aberdovey in North Wales. Since we were sending pupils to these schools, it seemed reasonable to go and have a look at the places and talk to the people in charge there. So I went on a very pleasant and educational inspection trip and afterwards I wrote a report on it and recommended a few changes. Things were brought up to date and there was a Company decision for continued involvement with the scheme. They were good schemes and very good training in leadership qualities for teenagers.

Effective presentations

I went back in my mind to that incident in a pub in Belmullet and the bizarre and shameful story of the Company's communications with its travellers. The key word was 'communications'. What could I do about it?

Well, for a start, I had been observing Guinness personnel of all grades and classifications getting up in front of groups of people and making presentations on some Company matter. Sometimes they used visuals, sometimes not. The general standard of presentations was lamentable. It was a form of communications at which Guinness personnel were almost uniformly bad. What to do about it? The answer was training.

So I went and did a bit of travel and investigated what was on offer by way of training in this subject both in Ireland and the UK, where I signed on for two courses on training. I decided we could do as well if not better at St James's Gate. So I designed a course, called it 'Effective Presentations', and proceeded to market it within the Company.

It was a two-day, full-time course with not more than six people on each course. Each participant would make four presentations during the course. These presentations would be video-recorded and assessed and criticised by the others on the course. We had a few tentative enquiries, and then our first course.

Afterwards I did some 'tweaking' here and there to tidy up loose ends and improve things but basically the course was well received. Little did I know then that, after a slowish start, it was to run around the Company like wildfire and was used by all sections of personnel from the top downwards. It also spread out in other directions in that, for one thing, whenever a member of top management was due to give what he considered to be an important presentation either inside or outside the Company he often practised it with me in the Training Centre. We tightened up on unnecessary flapdoodle. We simplified and clarified some visuals and/or designed some new ones. We got the timing right.

In time, that led to some script writing by me so that the style and content suited the particular audience involved. And we settled basic questions at rehearsals such as 'What exactly do you want to achieve by making this particular presentation and why do you want to achieve it?'

When I left the Company in 1978, one of my products which I took to the marketplace was the course in 'Effective Presentations'. Over the years, as a communications consultant, I have conducted this course all over Ireland (both inside and outside St James's Gate), in the UK, in several European countries, and in North America. Truly, great oaks from little acorns grow! And truly this product has yielded considerable dividends and job satisfaction.

Pre-retirement training

The next thing we did in the Training Department was to examine what we were offering to people retiring from the Company. There was a course already in operation, but part of my job was to review it and see if it should be changed in any way. In fact it was a good course, with expert advice about things like health, exercise, diet, pensions, banking, holidays, gardening, wills, part-time education and so on. We did a little adjustment here and there and the course has been of great help to all grades of personnel on their retirement. Again it was based on the Guinness point of view that if you had spent most or all of your working life in the Company, then you were entitled to be given some help with how to deal with your retirement.

Dealing with the media

Another part of my job was to help top management to cope with interviews — for TV, radio, newspapers, magazines. At the time I was doing a lot of interviewing on radio and TV and when a director was invited to do an interview or to participate in a broadcast programme my job was to put him through his paces. We set up a studio in the Training Centre, bought the necessary camera and other gear, and used a member of our photographic section on camera, lighting and audio.

Again this exercise was a useful training for people who were to represent the Company with the media. Not only did it familiarise them with the routine of studio work but it often resulted in clarification of what should be said and how to say it effectively in a matter of a very few minutes.

Internal videos

Using our TV gear we also made some videos for use within the Company. One example. There was an outbreak of back problems being suffered by men in departments where the lifting and handling of heavy items was not being done correctly, which meant men were developing back problems, having to go on sick leave and maybe needing fairly lengthy series of expensive treatments by our physiotherapist.

How to train the men to lift heavy items correctly? The answer was to make a video showing how not to do it and why not. And then how to do it correctly and why. Drawing on the expertise of our physiotherapist and bringing our own scripting and video-making experience to bear, we made a video that proved very helpful and was much used in the Company.

The fretful midge

There were all sorts of other courses going on all the time in the Training Centre in which I was not involved but, not for the first time with me, every course I was involved in setting up lost its challenge for me when it got to the stage of running smoothly and well. On the other hand the communications courses in which I was the trainer/ lecturer/tutor always presented me with wholesome challenges which I thrived on and enjoyed. Each new group of trainees, both as individuals and as a class, always presented me with a fascinating exercise in things like their attitude to training, hang-ups, fears, moods, expectations, faults, pluses, interaction capabilities etc. I have always claimed that a worthwhile 'trainer' will always learn from a class. I know I did.

In all modesty I think it fair to mention that many companies and several training/educational organisations came to see us and to examine how we did things. It was taken as a very nice compliment to us and the spreading of the gospel of the efficacy of training gave us a great kick and, as we learned, helped other people to set up courses and manage their own training needs.

And then two things happened, both of which were good for me. One was that the old fretful midge started inside me again and I just had to get out of second gear and into fourth. *Mirabile dictu*, and with fine synchronisation, things in the Company were coming to a head and there was a place for me on the team that was trying to put things right. Instead of walking into one new job, I walked into two. One was setting up a new Internal Communications Unit, and the other was being in charge of another brand-new operation, the Voluntary Parting Scheme. I was back in fourth gear!

Dry Rot in a Brewery

The question is often asked by Guinness people, 'What ever happened to our lovely Company that it found itself in the mess it eventually got into?' Books have been written about that, and I don't intend to rewrite them. Nevertheless, this is a question we should consider here. And to do that, we need to go back to the end of World War II and the beginning of vast changes for the world, including for Guinness.

No living thing can exist without reference to the environment in which it lives. Likewise with organisations – including Guinness. And the environment in which Guinness found itself living in those forty years (1938–78) was truly extraordinary by any standards. When an atomic bomb destroyed the city of Hiroshima in 1945, humanity realised for the first time that all living matter on this planet could be destroyed in a single day. The surrender of Japan to the Allied forces some weeks later was the end of the greatest and bloodiest conflict ever, in which 55 million people had been killed and countless millions wounded. The total material cost of the war was put at $1.5 million million – which was more than the total material cost of all previous wars put together.

Nearer home we saw most of Europe in smithereens, towns and cities bombed to bits. The UK had also been extensively damaged by bombings. The country and its people were spent – in all senses of that word. The British Empire was broke and on the way to disintegration. Even in neutral Ireland we had suffered serious shortages of various foodstuffs, fuels, power, clothes, jobs. Eventually, and like the rest of the world, Ireland had to shake itself as if out of a stupor, to look at our changed surroundings and to take the first tentative steps towards rehabilitation and change.

Within this chaotic global and local environment the staid and reliable St James's Gate looked at itself in a mirror and was not exactly enamoured of what it saw. To be sure, it had survived the all-pervading hostile environment of the last few years but, not only did the place require a massive re-cranking, but even the mirror itself was in need of replacement. What changes were necessary inside the walls?

Improving production

To begin with, the product needed attention, from a scientific and production angle and particularly in areas such as sterilisation. Back from the war had come a Guinness Brewer named Launce McMullan who was ideally qualified to spearhead the production team. He had been serving in the Royal Navy Volunteer Reserve (RNVR) in Scotland when two things happened. One was that, during the war, the Americans had decided that since many of their overseas-based troops were unable to get their hands on beer, the thing to do was build a brewery in a ship and sail it all over the place to quench the thirsts. They then discovered that there was a brewer in the RNVR in Scotland and before he knew what was happening to him our man was in Vancouver helping in the conversion of the 11,000-ton Blue Funnel liner *Menestheus* into Fleet Amenity

Ship *Menestheus* – the first brewery-ship or floating brewery in the world. However, just when it had completed its trials and had succeeded in brewing excellent beer, the war ended before it got under way.

Back came McMullan to St James's Gate and to the quality of the product. Under the general umbrella of sterilisation the brewing plant was under scrutiny and that included beer vessels such as vats plus the casks which carried the stout to wherever it should go. Because wooden containers of any sort are notoriously difficult to sterilise adequately, the whole area of production, packaging and transport of the product was ear-marked for dismantling and replacement with metal containers. That meant time, effort, expertise and millions of pounds to be spent.

Effects of the war on personnel

Personnel shared the top of the list of things which were changing and requiring attention. In July 1953 the personnel picture at St James's Gate showed the following:

Staff 537
Trades 543
Non-trades 2756
Total (active) 3836
Pensioners 1743

One of the main problems had to do with a new and strange mood in the place. People who had not gone to war began to notice an element of destabilisation and restiveness in those who had come back. Many of them had come back to find themselves again wearing dungarees and rolling casks. Somehow or other it was a very disappointing anticlimax. What had it all been about?

As in the 1914–18 war, the Company had certainly kept its side of the severance and return terms. So had the men. But they had been through the mill. And although they had been used to normal company discipline before they went away, and in the forces while they were away, they seemed to want to shrug off any signs of discipline now that they were back. They wanted a dog to kick. The Company and its practices were an obvious choice.

We had to remember that, but for the sacrifices made by such men as these, it might well have been that none of us would have had peace, let alone a job. I might well have found myself in their situation if my attempt to join the Royal Air Force had not been aborted. All that said, it is worth while comparing the attitude of the Company and indeed that of Irish people in general to those who served in the 1914–18 war with those who served in the 1939–45 war.

In the 1914–18 war, before Ireland became independent, over eight hundred employees of the Guinness company served in the British forces. Scattered all over the world, they served on land, on sea and in the air. They held the belief that they were giving their service for the defence of the British Empire (of which Ireland at the time was a part) and for the freedom of small nations. One hundred and three of those eight hundred never came back.

No grade or rank of employees of the Company is absent from the Roll of Honour which was produced after that war to commemorate those who had served. While these men were away, they were paid by the forces at whatever the going rate was. In addition, the Company paid half of their wages or salaries to their families and their jobs were guaranteed when they returned. And shortly after their return we find an example of the mood of the times that were in it then. On 16 February 1920, a deputation of demobbed Brewery workmen waited upon the chairman of the Company and presented an illuminated address consisting of the following words:

> *We, the employees of Messrs. A. Guinness Son and Company Limited who left their employment to serve in His Majesty's Forces in the late European War, hereby tender our sincere thanks to the Directors and Board of the Firm for their unfailing generosity and kindness to us, our wives and families, during our absence on Service, and for their patriotic action in keeping open and reinstating their employees in the positions they occupied previous to the War. We assure the Directors and Board of our grateful loyalty and devotion to the interests of the Company.*

There followed a list of all those on the Company's books who had joined up.

In reply to the above the chairman, the Earl of Iveagh, addressed the deputation as follows:

My friends,

I am anxious, in the first place, to express the pleasure it affords me to meet you here today, recognising, as I do, the friendly spirit which has induced you and those you have been working with to prepare and submit the kind and flattering address which you have just presented. It will always be valued as showing the friendly feelings existing between the Board and those of our Employees who volunteered to go and fight for those of us at home, in the Great War.

Need I say how glad we are to have this opportunity of personally telling you how much we appreciated your patriotic spirit in voluntarily going out to face the dangers and hardships you went through, and how much we rejoice to see you back with us safe and well.

I am proud to think that in all my long life there have been no misunderstandings or troubles as between us and those who have worked for us and so loyally with us in the past. I earnestly trust that in the future those happy relations will always be continued.

I again thank you heartily on my own behalf and on behalf of the others members of the Board.

My personal interest in this particular episode in the Company's history was that my father, Edward Byrne fought in the 1914–18 war. My father and two of his brothers, Thomas and Richard, got jobs in the Guinness company and so were part of the list of men who were involved in the events recorded above.

How changed was all that from the scene in 1945/6 when Ireland was a Republic and those who had volunteered to serve with the Allies were virtually ignored when they came back. Indeed, in some cases, they were actually condemned for doing what they did. Small wonder then that they were at a loss to know just how to think and feel about things. And this mood of bewilderment was becoming infectious. It was not substantially helped by the intake in the late 1940s and early 1950s of people who had not been in Guinness before the war but were now taken on partly because they were needed and partly because the Company wanted to play its part in the overall rehabilitation of war veterans. They too found it difficult to settle into this extraordinary world inside St James's Gate. The fact that the Company took on some members of the Irish defence forces as well as those from the British forces did little, but something, to help matters.

Enter Sir Charles Harvey

So this feeling of surly and smouldering indiscipline was common in the Company and the question was how to fix it. Gradually, things reached Board level. There we find a master stroke by the Board in its post-war appointment of Sir Charles Harvey as Director in Charge of Personnel. He was ideal for the job. Very tall, very lean and in his early sixties, he had retired as a major general in the British army after a lifetime as a soldier. He understood dealing with men and he was excellent at it.

He saw a situation where, at shop-floor level, the craftsmen were unionised and industrial relations between them and management were reasonably good. Admittedly there were over twenty separate unions to deal with and, although these were represented within six main groupings, none of the major groupings was prepared to discuss issues jointly. The non-trades personnel were not unionised and therefore there did not exist a mandate from any sub-group to represent them in discussions with management. As for staff – unionisation never occurred to them. Well, not yet. As if to stave off the day, the Board set up the Staff Investigatory Committee (of which I was vice-chairman) to tell the Company what complaints the staff had and how they should be put right.

The whole area of personnel required fairly urgent and major treatment in order to get relations working smoothly. As we'll see later, the inevitable happened and virtually all personnel eventually became unionised – a situation undreamt of in a place which had always been thought of as offering the best jobs in industry and with an impeccable industrial relations record.

Sir Charles got cracking and things started to happen. It started with an attempt to form what was called the Guinness Association, to represent non-trades personnel.

That failed. It was replaced by the Guinness Employees Organisation in 1948. That was better – but not good enough. Finally came the Workers Union of Ireland and, by 1960, almost all non-craft workers were members. Who would ever have guessed it? What a come-down for 'the aristocracy of the Dublin working classes'!

In the early 1960s came a major breakthrough with the productivity agreement between management and the Workers Union of Ireland, which was followed shortly afterwards by a special agreement with the Company's skilled workers. These agreements were hailed by both management and unions as an historic step forward in industrial relations.

Harvey had some excellent ideas and his own particular manner and style helped enormously. One of his more bizarre operations was to hold a series of those genteel entertainments popular in the 1920s and 1930s called *thés dansants*. Traditionally afternoon tea parties, these functions were held at four in the afternoons in the Guinness residence in James's Street. They were hosted by Sir Charles and Lady Harvey and were for a mixture of male and female staff members. As you might imagine, the dance band was made up of very talented Guinness personnel – and tea partly replaced by Guinness. They went on for two hours and, while in retrospect it might sound like a mad idea, at the time they were generally considered to be a breakthrough in the almost traditional stand-offishness between male and female staff. Who would ever think that part of one's duties as a Guinness employee was to attend a *thé dansant*?

Changes in the marketplace

Outside the walls, in the marketplace, changes were going on also, and the Company was dealing with them. Our transport systems were being modernised. We were moving from prams and horses to mechanised and bulk transport – not just using what was available but actually designing revolutionary new methods and vessels unknown to the outside world.

Apart from buying up ale breweries and building a new lager brewery, we bought some pubs. There were two reasons for these purchases. An overseas brewer had put his nose into the Irish market and had started looking at small Irish breweries and some licensed premises. This could have become a threat to Guinness in its own back yard. So a move was made and the stranger withdrew.

A second reason for buying pubs was that we knew little about the retail side of our business. Once we sold the product to the licensee and got paid, we were not involved in the financial or business side of the publican's work. After the war, we realised that this was not good enough. We should know about all aspects of the licensed trade. So we bought and managed pubs.

GGSI

One of the most revolutionary and important things the

Company did was to set up, in 1965, a company called Guinness Group Sales (Ireland) Ltd – known simply as GGSI. These newly acquired ale and lager breweries all had their own sales and marketing teams and, when they all came in under the large Guinness umbrella, silly things began to happen. For instance, it often happened that the sales representatives for lager, ale and stout met in the same town and even in the same pub at the same time to do their separate business. Wholly unnecessary expenditure. Why not just one person to represent all products in the group?

Personnel snags

Well, there were personnel snags and the manner of their solution is yet another example of the way the Guinness company operated when it came to dealing with people.

There were Guinness travellers all over the country and all of them, one way or another, had been absorbed into the No. 1 Staff and enjoyed all its terms and privileges. People on the outdoor sales staff of all the other companies that had been bought up by Guinness were known as sales reps. They were professional sales people with considerable experience and expertise in the business of selling. Guinness travellers knew little about such matters – they didn't have to know; it was not part of their brief.

The salaries and expenses allowed to travellers exceeded those of the sales reps. How to bring them all into one fold with similar terms of reference about the work to be done plus equal pay and allowances for equal work done? And there was that thing about 'outsiders' and the No. I Staff. Clubland raised its head again.

Eventually that was all resolved and the problem about the No. I Staff was settled by an interesting ploy – don't bother about it and it might go away! Well, it wasn't bothered about and, whatever about theory, the practice resulted in the salient fact that it wasn't allowed to matter. In fact it was one of the first series of cherished bricks to be dislodged in the wall of hierarchical personnel structures in the expanding organisation. Truly things were beginning to change and with gathering speed.

In fact GGSI simply looked at all of its products to be marketed and sold in the Republic of Ireland and set up appropriate departments within GGSI (each with its own boss) to maximise the selling and profits of the entire range. Almost every production company under the umbrella of the Guinness organisation went about its business of producing whatever their product was and they then paid GGSI a fee for marketing and selling that product. It was as simple as that. It was the new style of management which was so different from the old and which was part of worldwide changes in doing almost everything. Another fall-out of World War II.

Change or die

So the whole world was changing. The environment in which Guinness had been operating for so long was changing. It was a case of change or die. Meantime, despite the changes going on within the walls, and the adjustments being made to meet and thrive in the changing environment in which we operated, we were still not really a very well company.

In the 1960s, the Guinness Group consisted of three main companies – our parent company based in London and its two off-spring, a brewery and company at St James's Gate in Dublin and a brewery and company at Park Royal in London.

The family business had long since (1886) become a public company, and, although there was still a member of the family in the chair, the Board of Directors in all three companies was composed mostly of people from outside the family. This was no change from the long-established Guinness tradition of having outsiders like the Pursers, Geoghegans and La Touche at top level, with a Guinness in the driving seat. Many of these outsiders were extremely competent, professional businessmen. At all events, the Dublin Company in the 1960s seemed to be in good hands and all seemed to be reasonably well. But was it?

Influence of Sir Hugh Beaver

In our parent company in London, Sir Hugh Beaver, who had been a great MD, retired in 1960 after a heart attack, having been only thirteen years in office. A lot of what Beaver did by way of diversification was bold, sensible and successful (especially in Ireland); however, other diversification activities drifted off into disaster and substantial loss. This has been attributed, at least in part, to the view that those who were running Guinness at the time had little idea of modern management and they wrongly assumed that because they knew how to run a brewery successfully they could do likewise with companies outside brewing. Well, they couldn't. And they didn't.

Disquiet in the 1960s

Beaver shared the MD job with Lord Boyd for two years prior to his retirement and when he left in 1960, Boyd took over.

Apart from vague feelings of unease about the poor performance of diversifications, there was a growing disquiet about the parent company's overall performance. Some figures illustrate the reason for this. They show profit after tax results as follows:

1960 £4.61m

1961 £4.24m

1962 £4.23m

1963 £4.23m

1964 £4.79m

Not exactly exciting growth results.

One morning in the late 1960s (I suspect it was a cold, wet, inclement Monday morning in February), the Company woke up to the fact that the cost of producing a barrel of stout at St James's Gate was twice the cost (or even more) of producing a barrel of beer in European breweries.

So if the Company continued to produce beer in Dublin, then it would have to increase its selling price in order to stay in business.

An increase of the required order in the selling price, however, would result in a reduction in sales and that would lead to a reduction in profits. And reduction in profits might well lead to loss of confidence in the Dublin Company to fulfil its export trade, and we'd be lucky if we even survived as a small local brewery catering only for the Irish trade.

The future looked horrendous. But what to do? The answer was that all costs, and especially the very high personnel costs, had to be cut drastically. And not in the long term, but very urgently.

Development Plan Mark 1

The first move was to set up a meeting to discuss the crisis and to decide on what action to take. The main guiding principle was the question 'How do we reach world standards of competitiveness at the least cost, financial and otherwise, to all who work here?' The result was what was known as Development Plan Mark I. It was the first of several such plans. It was discussed and negotiated with all twenty-three trade unions in the Company and the terms were more or less agreed. It was a start.

It meant that every single operation or practice or system within the Dublin company had to be scrutinised to identify wastage and eliminate it. To take an example. The brewing plant at St James's Gate was itself old and inefficient and needed a very large labour force to operate it and maintain it in working order. New, modern plant was urgently required to cope with all stages of the brewing process with maximum effectiveness and efficiency. (In this case efficiency was defined as producing the maximum results at the minimum cost.)

So, between 1971 and 1991 the Company spent over £150m on this mammoth task. The work eventually resulted in turning St James's Gate into one of the most modern and efficient brewing plants in the world.

The Brewery Council

Then came disagreement between the unions and management about how to share the gains of the Development Plan. Tempers and temperatures rose rapidly. The culmination of the increasingly rancorous situation was a strike at St James's Gate in 1974 – the first strike in the 215 years of the Company's existence. The unthinkable had happened. It had a most traumatic effect on everyone in the Company.

A thorough review of the Company's personnel structures, policies and problems was carried out, and a decision was taken that the Company would adopt a less secretive, more open and more participative style of management. The way to do this was to persuade all personnel into a greater sense of participation in the running of the Company. In June 1975 the Company organised a seminar to discuss involvement of employees.

The result of this was the publication of proposals for substantial involvement and the setting up of a representative working party to explore how involvement would work. That gave birth to the formation of the Brewery Council on 3 October 1977.

The Council consisted of twenty-one members. Twenty came from the seven employment categories (including management), plus a chairman. It has been described as 'the best example of voluntary disclosure in Ireland which has led to a significant increase in understanding the Company's affairs'. Management had learned a hard lesson. That Council, with its successes and its failures, is still in existence. As of writing it is twenty-two years old – a relatively short space of time in which to change a culture of 240 years.

The Voluntary Parting Scheme

An important part of the development plan was substantial reductions in personnel. Partly because of out-moded plant, and partly because of the plethora of non-essential servicing jobs like waiters, lavatory clerks, office-clock winders, guides and suchlike, there needed to be a reduction in personnel. A plan was designed which eventually resulted in a reduction of active service personnel from 4000 in 1953 to less than 1000 in 1991.

True to Guinness traditions, nobody was to be sacked.

The Company took into account what was called 'natural wastage' (one of the expressions I most dislike). By that was meant people who died and those who reached normal retirement age would not be replaced. Secondly, a plan was designed and put on offer. It was called the 'Voluntary Parting Scheme' and it was designed to offer very attractive departure terms for anyone who wanted to accept them. The scheme offered free retraining in almost any trade or profession (for example lorry-driving, pub management, taxi-ownership, oboe-playing were amongst the list), plus all the usual perks which any retired person normally enjoyed, like pension and free medical care, plus a golden handshake.

I was given the job of marketing this plan inside the walls. The place shuddered with disbelief. This Company, safe and solid, trusty and honourable for over two centuries, was now trying to persuade its people to get out long before their normal time of retirement. True, they were being offered a generous deal. But that wasn't really the point. They were being asked – persuaded – to accept that, in order to save St James's Gate, it was necessary to carry out this distressing major culling. For all of us it was the end of something we had accepted as a norm, to wit that Guinness was indestructible, immutable, steadfast. We, the personnel, could and did change and grow old and we knew we had to go when we reached the age of sixty-five. But the place itself – never!

These were very difficult times for all personnel. Before our very eyes we were watching the accelerating change of our much loved and respected Company into a hard-nosed, tough, impersonal factory. It was becoming a stranger to us. There was the face of sour efficiency about it. Everybody realised that drastic changes were absolutely necessary for survival but that didn't always assuage the hurt of watching what was happening as a result of the changes. We were about to leave our home from home. Leave our chums and friends. Leave our own particular part of St James's Gate and our job. How were we going to get on without it? What were we going to do all day every day now that we wouldn't be coming into St James's Gate? In fact, several people offered to remain on and do the work they were doing with no other payment than that on offer via the Voluntary Parting Scheme. Put another way, they were willing to work for nothing – anything rather than leave!

But, since the place was undergoing a metamorphosis perhaps it was better to leave than to stay? After all there's always a right time to leave even the best of parties. If our own image of it was now changing for ever it was futile to want to stay on in this different place. It had lost its heart and its very soul. To be sure, walking out the gate for the last time was indescribably sad. But staying on in this strange, insensitive, unpredictable place would be even worse. This was the kind of conversation I had with many a person who came to talk to me about the pros and cons of the scheme. I was completely sympathetic and empathetic. We were all sad and a little afraid. I freely admit that that took a lot out of me emotionally.

But in the end the target departures figures were achieved and stage one of the scheme was closed. It would be followed by a succession of somewhat similar schemes but, for the moment, the haemorrhage of departures was stemmed. It was goodbye to very good friends and colleagues.

Telling It

One result of all the mayhem that was going on in the company was a cascade of rumours, gossip, exaggeration and lies. It was absolutely essential that everyone should be told the facts – and told them as a matter of urgency. Communicating these details to all and sundry was obviously a *sine qua non* towards achieving the Company's goals without unnecessary further disturbance.

The Internal Communications Unit

So the Company set up a new Internal Communications Unit and I was it. This was a senior management post and my job was to keep all personnel fully informed about things they should know about. It included taking over the editorship of the Company's monthly house journal or newsletter and the publication of more frequent and urgent circulars and notices as the need arose. I couldn't help remembering that day in a pub in Belmullet...

I have what amounts almost to an obsession about the importance of effective internal communications in the running of an organisation. If you leave people in the dark about what's going on in the place then, *ipso facto*, you invite on the scene mischief-makers like rumour, gossip and downright lies. That, in turn, leads to confusion, uncertainty and a lowering of morale. And it serves you right!

At St James's Gate there was a system whereby people got to know things about the Company's operations which were of interest to them. For a very long time this

THE *GUINNESS HARP*

On St Patrick's Day 1958 was born the *Guinness Harp*, the house magazine of St James's Gate. It was published about six times a year and it ran until the spring of 1972. It was organised and edited by the Company press officer, with the help of his staff plus an executive committee of some twelve people drawn from all ranks of personnel. From the word go it was a wonderful success. With an annual subscription of three shillings (or four shillings postage paid) it was some bargain.

To begin with, it covered virtually all aspects of the production, marketing and selling of all beer produced at St James's Gate and other Guinness-owned breweries in Ireland. It also included news of the establishment of Guinness breweries overseas, their sales, their marketing and their activities.

The *Harp* also covered news of the whole range of activities of Guinness people at work, at play, at home, at study, on holidays. From the time it was launched, the *Harp* opened its pages for use by every Brewery society and every sporting activity in the Company. Births, marriages and deaths were announced. Promotions, retirements, new entrants were listed.

Every aspect of the running of St James's Gate was explained to readers. New equipment, new production processes, new inventions — all got a write-up. There were 'spies' out around the Brewery digging up fascinating stuff about the historical record of the old Brewery. Anecdotes, stories, adventures, reminiscences got space. Sporting achievements were highlighted — especially (as often happened) a member of the Company winning international honours. In short, anything that had to do with the workings of the Brewery and its product, or with anyone involved in this work was fair game for consideration as publication material.

But things did not end there. Flicking through the editions over its fourteen years of publication it is remarkable to read the constant stream of contributions from well-known writers in Ireland who were invited to send in material on all sorts of subjects. One wrote about the Guinness brewery in Malaysia; another wrote on some of the seabirds of the Saltees; there was an article about cricket lovers' eccentricities; about the Spanish Armada salvage expedition in the Blasket Sound; on the place of the pub in Irish sport; on Goya's painting 'Lady in a Black Mantilla'.

Alas, by 1972, such attractive but costly side-lines came under the dreaded 'cut-backs' scrutiny and *Harp* ceased publication. It was sadly missed.

information percolated down via such conduits as notice-boards, circulars, Board Orders – and the Brewery taps about which I have written. But, to put it mildly, the whole operation of internal communications was a hit-and-miss affair. There was nobody actually in charge of it so, because it was everyone's business, it was nobody's business. And the situation wasn't helped in knowing that our junior sibling brewery in Park Royal had their house magazine in operation for ten years – but we had no such thing. Something had to be done. And it was.

St James's Gate Newsletter

A new monthly magazine called the *St James's Gate Newsletter* was launched in October 1972. It was quite different from the previous magazine, the *Guinness Harp*, which had ceased publication six months previously. Peripheral activities were gone, though everything to do with personnel at work and at play was kept, and the emphasis was turned in on the Company's problems and their solution. As with the *Harp*, the new magazine was under the control of the press office.

That lasted from October 1972 to February 1973 when the Board announced the establishment of the new post of internal communications officer and, logically, control of *Newsletter* was transferred to me. I edited the magazine until August 1976, when I went on to concentrate on other aspects of internal communications.

Newsletter fitted in with all the other strands of internal communications being set up and operated and it became one of the main channels of news and views between management and personnel – and *vice versa*. And since the place was undergoing major personnel changes at the time this tried to keep everyone informed of all relevant developments, as they happened. As with the *Harp*, our own Guinness Printing Department did all the professional work of layout, photos, format, printing etc on *Newsletter*, so it was truly a 'house' magazine.

For me, editing *Newsletter* was a very important item in the portfolio of jobs to be done in internal communications. I had freedom to talk to anyone about anything which might be used in *Newsletter*.

Every edition had a particular page set aside for letters from Brewery personnel, and no holds were barred. Sometimes we had a few letters in. Sometimes just one. Sometimes not even one – so we went to press with a blank page, because we insisted on maintaining an open door for anyone to say what was on their mind about what was going on. That way, there were no grounds for complaints about inability to express opinions.

Moving on

By 1976 I had handed over the editing of *Newsletter*. I still worked in the Internal Communications area, but things were ticking over, and it was time for me to review my position once again. What was my future in the Company? I wondered. Should I go or stay? The answer took months to decide upon, but in the end, I decided to go.

I decided to go because the place I was now working in was no longer the place I had grown to love and be happy in. There didn't seem to me to be any strong prospects of worthwhile promotion or change. Many of my chums had gone, and it was lonely without them. Outside the Brewery the scenario was very much brighter. There was a lot going on in radio and television broadcasting. It was very exciting and challenging. There was a place waiting for me there. It was also financially far more rewarding than Guinness. And besides, in my case, I was offered consultancy work with the Company which, as it turned out, went on for almost twenty years after I left. So I would be saved the trauma of the major surgery of leaving – walking out the gate for good.

Finally, in April 1978, I 'left'. I had my farewell party. On the following Monday morning I was back in for a meeting. On the Monday afternoon I was recording a book programme in RTÉ. I was off!

Epilogue

And now I'm coming to the end of my odyssey. I've tried to tell part of the story of a phenomenon. It is sad to write about the demise of this Company as it once was – an independent, privately owned then public company controlled at the top by members of the Guinness family. It was out on its own producing a stout which now accounts for a staggering 80% of all stouts sold throughout the world. It also produced other beers which are marketed to a very satisfactory degree of sales and profits. It retained a small number of worthwhile diversifications.

So why the sadness in writing about it? What went wrong? Did something go wrong? It is beyond the scope of this book to go into any great details about what happened post-1978, and at least one book has already been written about the matter. What can be said here is perhaps best expressed by a few statistics.

The parent company's results for 1980 and 1981 showed trading profits of £49.5m and £45.5m respectively. Not good – and getting worse. Things were on the slide. Something had to be done. Looked at as a patient, the Company was not well. It needed specialist care. There was, it seems, nobody within the Company sufficiently qualified or deemed capable of providing it. So they went out into the marketplace and found a Company doctor. His name was Ernest Saunders. He came into the Company in October 1981 at a starting salary of £73,000 a year.

By 1983 the Guinness Company declared net assets of £251.9m. By the time it acquired Bells Distilleries in 1985, and then the Distillers Company (the largest Scotch whisky distiller in the world) in 1986, declared net assets of the Company were £1049m. Guinness was now in the big league of selling alcoholic drinks (besides beer). These acquisitions were spearheaded by Saunders and the deals stopped the Guinness 'slide' and turned things around.

A good thing, apparently. The trouble was that, in doing all this, Saunders was indicted on a criminal charge in connection with the Company's financial dealings. He was sacked from Guinness in January 1987. Four months later he was arrested, became the central figure in a famous court case, was found guilty and sent to jail. The boss of Guinness in jail! And while the old girl survived all this, the stainless image of Guinness had had a sizeable dollop of mud flung at it and, some say, never quite recovered from the macula.

In December 1997, the expanded Company entered into a merger with GrandMet to form the behemoth Diageo plc. Diageo is now one of the world's leading consumer goods companies with an annual turnover of £12 billion, an operating profit (before exceptional items) of £1942m and total net assets of £21.8 billion. Guinness and its products are in there and doing very well. Shareholders are delighted. The future looks rosy. So what's the problem? Well, not exactly a problem more a feeling of sentimental regret pour les temps perdus.

To put that simply: in the inexorable march of time, almost all things change. Guinness is one such. Gone are its old-world charm and personality. Like all human endeavours it had its faults – but then nothing done by humans is faultless. Whatever else, the Company had immense charm and style, and it is sad to see how much it has changed. Its personality generated fun, friendships, caring, decency, warmth, honour, harmony, honesty. It was a workplace which was a club. And members of that club had an indefinable but real bond with each other, which was recognised and admired both by those inside and those outside the Company. It is difficult to imagine anyone who was in the Company before or during the period 1938–78 walking out the gate at retirement without feeling quite emotional about it. At any rate, I felt very sad.

Fortunately for me, I was back in there doing communications consultancy work for some years after voluntary retirement so I was, as it were, in touch. But it was not the same. I had no office, no base, no job. The umbilical had been cut. I was unattached, with no berth. Worse still, I watched woefully the pleasant little things about the place disappearing one by one, being whittled away. And being replaced by efficiency, competency, adaptability, vigour, aptitude – qualities needed to deal effectively with the changed and changing world out there in the marketplaces of the world.

When I was researching material for this book I went again to St James's Gate. I had done quite a bit of acting with the Guinness Players and elsewhere and driving in through the Front Gate in 1998 was like walking on to a stage. The props were all more or less where they had always been. The place was its usual tidy, clean self. But where were the people? The few I saw were not members of the cast. They were strangers. I knew none of them. None of them knew me. No greetings were exchanged. No 'lines' swapped. It was quite unreal – nightmarish, as I found myself wandering in familiar surroundings but peopled by unknowns.

In the offices, however, I found several old friends. We did our work and we exchanged pleasantries, anecdotes, fun. It was a bit like old times – but only a bit. These chums were cast members and we knew and exchanged our lines. But back out in the Brewery Yard I again saw these strangers. Driving out the Front Gate involved a compulsory (and sensible) inspection of my car boot to ensure I was not stealing anything. Again that 'can't understand what's happened' bit.

Over the period of my service with the Company, figures for the total yearly output of Guinness from St James's Gate rose from 560 million pints in 1938 to 638 million in 1978. That represents an increase in annual production of almost 80 million pints during those forty years. Spread over the period and in round figures, that is an average increase in production of two million pints a year, or 5460 pints a day, or almost four pints a minute.

So, to end on a whimsical note, it is idle but harmless, to speculate about what contribution I – or indeed anyone working for the Company for a comparable period – made over those forty years to that increased production rate of four pints a minute. A sobering thought – though that is not a very appropriate adjective to use in a book on the subject of Guinness. At any rate, production did not decrease over my time with the Company, so perhaps after all it can be assumed that at worst my presence there did not impede progress.

That may not be – nor is it meant to be – a very scientific conclusion, but at least it's a comforting thought with which to end. Cheers!

Appendix:
The Guinness Family

The story of Guinness is the story of a nobody who became a somebody, an Irishman in a tiny village in Ireland who brewed a beer and founded a brewery that became the largest brewery in the world and who marketed that beer in such a way that it became the most famous beer in the world.

In doing what he did, Arthur Guinness became wealthy. Members of the dynasty he founded are immensely wealthy. Their wealth is locked up in trusts with the result that it is impossible for any of the beneficiaries to take out more than they are entitled to have. And such are the investments that the interest earned by them is enough to keep the beneficiaries among the world's richest — almost without touching the seed corn. They can't stop getting richer by the pico-second.

In addition to the acquisition of wealth, the man himself and his descendants became famous. Many of them reached the heights of ennoblement and made their way into the top echelons of almost all aspects of life on this planet — social, academic, sporting, political, military, the arts.

In the course of becoming successful and wealthy, this family has left countless examples of its philanthropic work in Ireland and abroad. Both the family and the Company were extremely generous and left their indelible, unique and ubiquitous mark on all aspects of life in Ireland.

To tell the story of the Guinness family adequately would take a whole book and many years of research, and in any case the history of the Guinness family has long since been written. So here I present just the briefest sketches of the six family members who ran the company between 1759 and 1986 (dates are birth and death):

Arthur I	1725–1803
Arthur II	1768–1855
Sir Benjamin Lee, first baronet	1798–1868
Edward Cecil, first Lord Iveagh	1847–1927
Rupert Edward Cecil, second Lord Iveagh	1874–1967
Arthur Francis Benjamin, third Lord Iveagh	1937–1992

Between them, these men were in control of the Guinness Brewery at St James's Gate for the 227 years between 1759 and 1986, and the story of the phenomenal success of the brewing side of the Guinness family points to the superb business acumen and very hard work of these six men. They were shrewd, energetic, sensible, balanced, of sound judgement, ambitious, creative, honourable, fair.

The very beginning

Once upon a time, hundreds of years ago, a gentleman called Arthur Price was the Protestant Archbishop of Cashel. He lived in Oakleigh Park House, at a village called Celbridge in County Kildare. He employed a local called Richard Guinness whose job included the roles of agent, rent collector, receiver and factotum. Fortunately for the world, the inclusion of that word 'factotum' in his job description meant that, among other things, Richard had to

THE PRODUCT

The word 'beer' is a generic term for a range of alcoholic drinks that includes lager, ale, stout, porter, barley wine. Beer is usually made with water, malt, hops and yeast.

When Arthur Guinness started brewing at St James's Gate he produced only ale. That was because ale was the most common beer in Ireland and was the beer being produced by the hundreds of Irish breweries of that time. And not only by breweries. In the middle to late 1770s much of the beer consumed in Ireland was produced by publicans, a practice that is starting to be revived in recent years.

By the early 1770s, a new beer from London arrived on the Irish market. Because of the use of roasted barley, this new beer had an attractive dark colour. It was called 'porter', because it was very popular with London porters, men doing hard manual work who liked their beer to look strong and to be strong. They had quite a range to choose from with marvellous names like 'Pharoah', 'Huff-Cup' and 'Knockdown'. Eventually the name 'porter' became 'extra stout' which was eventually shortened to 'stout'

Arthur I was impressed by this imported porter and proceeded to brew some of it. He liked what he saw and drank. So did his customers. He brewed more of it. In May 1796 he shipped six and a half barrels of Guinness porter to London. He called it West India porter. This was the first time that St James's Gate exported any of its products. So successful was it that, by 1799, Arthur stopped brewing ale and concentrated his entire production on porter. It was to be one of the great decisions in the history of brewing. By the year 1800 production of porter at St James's Gate had reached an annual figure of 361,000 gallons.

do some ale-brewing for His Grace. Richard's son, Arthur, was to become one of the most famous men in the world.

Arthur Guinness I

The young Arthur Guinness probably went to the local school and then, in his spare time, helped his father to produce the table ale in the basement of the archbishop's house. That was Arthur's blessed (or at least para-ecclesiastical) introduction into the world of beer-brewing, and he never looked back.

Coming out of that Oakleigh Park basement one day in 1752, young Arthur discovered that Dr Price had just passed away and, in his will, had left £100 each to Richard

Guinness and to his son Arthur. That legacy allowed Arthur to lease a small brewery in nearby Leixlip, where he and his young brother Richard were launched on the commercial beer merry-go-round. The year was 1756. They were in business for only three years when Arthur decided to hand over the developing Leixlip operation to Richard, while he himself headed for Dublin and bigger things.

As it happened, there was a run-down, non-operating brewery at a place called St James's Gate — the ancient entrance to the city of Dublin from the south-west. There was a house and garden on the brewery site. The lease of the whole place was on offer at £45 a year and the term of the lease was 9000 years. With an eye to securing continuity of supplies and a shrewd feel for a bargain, Arthur signed on the dotted line. And so, in 1759, out of the tatty remains of a derelict brewery in James's Street, was born the St James's Gate Brewery, with the 34-year-old Arthur Guinness in command. It was to become the biggest and most famous brewery in the world.

As for Arthur himself, we have very little information about him, but we do have a wealth of data about what he did. For instance, apart from everything else, he left his wife more than enough to live well. His personal estate, valued at probate at about £25,000 (about £865,000 in today's money) went to his children. Not bad for a tradesman from a little village in Ireland at the beginning of the nineteenth century.

Of Arthur's ten surviving children (out of a total of

twenty-one), we know that three of them, Arthur II, Benjamin and William Lunell joined the Brewery. That started what has come to be known as 'the Guinnessty'.

The first Arthur Guinness died in 1803. He was 78 years old. He is buried in the family vault at Oughterard, Co Kildare. He was a great man.

Arthur Guinness II

The second Arthur Guinness was born in 1768 at St James's Gate. He was 35 years old when his father died. Because he had been working in the Company for many years, he was no neophyte to management or to brewing. When he took over as boss in 1803, the yearly sales of Guinness were 809,244 gallons. When he died 52 years later, annual sales had risen to 4,191,264 gallons. That 10 per cent per annum rate of increase during his period at the helm at St James's Gate is only one indication of Arthur II's achievements.

Among his other activities he became Governor of the Bank of Ireland, President of the Dublin Chamber of Commerce, a member of the Farming Society of Ireland, of the Ouzel Galley Society and of the Meath Hospital Board. The result of all this was that he became a very well-known public figure. Not only was he very well known, but also he was respected and liked. He was known to be a very religious man, honourable and immensely able, and a gentleman to boot.

When he was 25, Arthur Guinness II married a girl called Anne Lee. She was the daughter of Benjamin Lee, of Merrion, just outside Dublin. They had nine children. Anne Lee died when she was only 43 year sold, and four years later, Arthur, who was then 53, married the 38-year-old Maria Barker of Dublin. That marriage, which was without issue, lasted until Maria died 16 years later. Arthur did not marry for a third time.

Arthur Guinness II died at the age of 87. He had been working up to the last. He was an outstanding member of the Guinness family who played an important part in the growth and prosperity of the Guinnesses and their Brewery. As well as all his other achievements, and quite apart from what he put into the family trust funds, he left a personal estate worth £9 million in today's money. He also left his third son, Benjamin Lee Guinness, in charge of things at St James's Gate.

Benjamin Lee Guinness

When Benjamin Lee Guinness took over in 1855, he was 57 years old and had 41 years' service with the Company behind him. He served for another thirteen years. He married his uncle Edward's daughter, Elizabeth Guinness, and they had four children.

In 1851, Benjamin Lee Guinness was elected Lord Mayor of Dublin. *The Irish Times* gave this account of his inauguration:

It was conducted with more than ordinary civic pomp. The municipal procession altogether eclipsed anything that had been seen since the palmy days of the old 'Orange' corporation and the day, so far as business was affected, was to all intents observed as a holiday.

Benjamin Lee Guinness had a country house and estate at St Anne's in Clontarf, just north of Dublin, and he had his town house at 1 Thomas Street, on the Brewery premises. His next target was a beautiful palladian mansion at 80 St Stephen's Green, which was designed by the famous Richard Cassells and was, at the time, owned by Benjamin's son-in-law, Robert Beatty West. Poor West got into trouble and died in debt, and Benjamin bought the house from the Commissioners of Encumbered Estates at the knock-down price of £2500. He then bought the house next door to it and both houses were converted into one great mansion. (It is now the headquarters of the Department of Foreign Affairs, Iveagh House.) Then Benjamin went west and bought the splendid Ashford Estate in County Galway.

But it wasn't all simply acquisitiveness. From his personal fortune, Benjamin Lee Guinness donated £150,000 for the badly needed restoration of St Patrick's Cathedral and also the contiguous Marsh's Library in Dublin, and he gave large sums towards repairing and extending the Coombe Lying-in Hospital in the Liberties in Dublin.

It was Benjamin Lee Guinness who, in 1862, decided to adopt the O'Neill Harp (which now lives in a glass case in the Long Room in Trinity College Library) as the Guinness trademark, and it has been in use ever since. The harp, being the acknowledged crest of Ireland, stamps Guinness as essentially Irish.

And then there was a wedding. Benjamin Lee's only daughter Anne Lee married a man named William Conyngham, who was in holy orders and who eventually became Archbishop of Dublin. He was eleven years younger than Anne. He was also the eldest son of the third Baron Plunket, and when that worthy died, William became the fourth baron. This happy affair meant that, for the first time, a title was introduced into the Guinness family.

For some time, Benjamin Lee Guinness had been engaged in politics. In 1863, he was elected Conservative and Unionist member for Dublin city. For the extent and totality of his involvement in Irish life – business, philanthropic and political – he was rewarded with a baronetcy in 1867. Not bad for the descendants of a Celbridge ostler!

Sir Benjamin Lee Guinness died in 1868 at the age of 70. Apart from substantial expansion at St James's Gate while he was in control, his various other business interests and his deep involvement in political, religious, public and philanthropic affairs, he left a vast personal fortune which, at probate, was valued at £1.1 million, or about £65 million in today's money. If you look at a picture of the man, you will see a handsome, kindly, pleasing and noble face. He is buried in Mount Jerome Cemetery in Dublin.

Edward Cecil Guinness – First Lord Iveagh

The fourth Guinness to take over the driving seat at St James's Gate was Edward Cecil, who became first Lord Iveagh and, when he died, was reckoned to be the second wealthiest man in England (at that he point he was living in London).

Edward Cecil Guinness was born in 1847. He started work in the Brewery at the age of fifteen, and then was for some years a part-time student at Trinity, from which he graduated with a BA in 1870 and MA in 1872. He shared the top job for some years with his brother Sir Arthur E Guinness and when he took over sole command he was only 29 years old – albeit with the crucial help of their father's chief assistant John Tertius Purser. The business grew rapidly under Edward. When he took over in 1876, output at St James's Gate was just over 28 million gallons per annum and when he died in 1927, it was 75 million gallons. It was in Edward's time (October 1886) that the Company went public. The total share value at the time was £6 million, of which the family kept substantially over 50 per cent.

Continuing the family tendency towards inter-marriage, Edward married Adelaide Maria Guinness, and they produced three children. Among other things, Edward bought a sheep farm in New Zealand, an oilfield in Canada, an hotel in San Francisco and an office block in New York. At home, he bought that wonderful mansion, Farmleigh, on a 60-acre site on the River Liffey near Castleknock in County Dublin.

In 1889, he founded the Guinness Trust (later the Iveagh Trust), to create homes for artisans in Dublin. He paid for the erection of blocks of flats in Bride Street, Patrick Street and Kevin Street. Later he paid for houses to be built in Crumlin.

In 1891, Edward Cecil Guinness was raised to the peerage and took the title of Baron Iveagh of County Down. The name 'Iveagh' was associated with a Magennis family of County Down, and as far back as 1781, Arthur Guinness I was using the coat of arms of this family, which was one of the old clans of Ireland. It is not clear whether or not our Guinness family was in fact related to the Magennises or Iveaghs, but it is certainly true that the name Magennis can also be spelt McGuinness, and it is not a long way from that to Guinness.

In 1897 he spent £1500 (105,000 in today's terms) on a new ring of bells for St Patrick's Cathedral and he paid for the restoration of the bell tower of the cathedral. He sponsored the building of the Iveagh Ward at the Rotunda Hospital and in 1900 he built the Iveagh Market for Dublin Corporation at a cost of £100,000 (£7 million in today's money). He cleared the site and laid out the gardens surrounding St Patrick's and in 1905 he built the Iveagh Hostel and, in the following year, the Iveagh Baths. The cost of the hostel and baths, together with the Iveagh Play

Centre for local children, came to a total of £2.6 million in today's money.

Edward Cecil Guinness became Chancellor of Trinity College and presented some of his land for the building of University College Dublin at Earlsfort Terrace and St Stephen's Green. He presented some of his picture collection to the Municipal Art Gallery in Dublin, equipped Dublin military hospitals in the 1914–18 war, presented the Guinness employees with a very large sports grounds in Crumlin, and in 1903 and again in 1911 he gave the equivalent of £50,000 to mark royal visits to Dublin for distribution among the Dublin hospitals 'without religious distinction'.

In 1919, Baron Iveagh became the Earl of Iveagh, and he died in 1927 at almost 80 years of age.

Rupert Edward Cecil Lee Guinness, Second Lord Iveagh

When the first Lord Iveagh died, he left behind him three children, of whom the eldest, Rupert, inherited his title. (The others were the Hon. Arthur and Walter Edward, who became the first Lord Moyne.) Rupert Edward Cecil Lee Guinness was born in 1874 and in 1903 married Lady Gwendolen Onslow. They had two sons and three daughters.

Rupert was a fine oarsman and sailor and he had an abiding interest in science. His microscope, which he acquired in childhood, was his lifelong companion and he received several scientific awards, among them being made a Fellow of the Royal Society. He served in the House of Commons until his father's death and his coming into the title meant that he had to move to the Lords.

Rupert's major life-project was scientific farming. Standards of hygiene in farming were low early in the twentieth century, and bovine TB was rampant. Rupert put things right and was responsible for ending the appalling toll of TB on the children of Britain and elsewhere. In his kitchen at Pyrford Court in Surrey, Rupert invented a method of extracting methane gas from farmyard manure. In the first instance, he used this gas to fuel the ovens in his own kitchen, and later it was used as a fuel for farm tractors. He also discovered how to create a fertiliser from garden refuse and this led to the setting up of a company to manufacture the new product. This company came in under the general umbrella of Guinness subsidiaries.

It was Rupert Guinness who presented the house his grandfather had acquired on St Stephen's Green in Dublin to the Irish government. In 1931, he was one of the Guinness family members who gave financial support to the organisation that later became the Irish Cancer Society. He was behind the introduction, in 1949, of a non-contributory pension scheme for staff and employees of Guinness. He became Chancellor of Trinity College Dublin and contributed substantially to many projects of the college, including helping to build the Schools of Physics and Botany, endowing baths for women students, providing funds towards the women's hostel and furnishing Purser

House at Trinity Hall, and giving a large subscription to the New Library.

Rupert Guinness was Chairman of the Company, at a time when England experienced one of its greatest slumps ever. Inevitably, sales of Guinness suffered, and output from St James's Gate declined. Drastic action was needed, and the decision was made for the first time to advertise Guinness.

Two tragedies struck the family at around this time. Walter Edward Guinness, first Baron Moyne, Rupert's youngest brother, who had a distinguished career in both Houses of Parliament and a fine record in the public service and a distinguished army career, was assassinated in Cairo in 1944 by members of the Stern Gang. Three months later, Rupert's third child and heir to the title, Arthur Onslow Edward Guinness, Viscount Elveden, was killed in active service in Holland at the age of 33.

In 1948, when he was 74 years old, the second Lord Iveagh was honoured with the insignia of a Knight Companion of the Most Noble Order of the Garter, the most prestigious order of knighthood in Great Britain, which entitled him to put up his shield in St George's Hall in Windsor Castle.

Lord Iveagh remained on as Chairman until he was 88 years old. In 1962, he handed over office to his grandson, Benjamin, who was 25 years of age. Benjamin was to be the last Lord Iveagh to be Chairman of the Company. Rupert's wife Gwendolen died at the age of 85 and the following year, 1967, Rupert also died, at 93. He left a vast fortune, the bulk of which was transferred to family trusts to benefit his successors. As Antony says of Brutus in *Julius Caesar*, 'His life was gentle, and the elements so mixed in him that nature might stand up and say to all the world, This was a man.'

Arthur Francis Benjamin Guinness, Third Lord Iveagh

The third Lord Iveagh was born in London in 1937 and succeeded to the title in 1967. He was appointed to the Board of Guinness in 1958 and became Chairman in 1967. He was the last Guinness to serve in that capacity.

I worked with the third Lord Iveagh, being appointed his ADC on a project concerning European brewers for some months in 1969 and working with him subsequently in various business operations. It was a great pleasure for me to have worked with this descendant of the first Arthur Guinness, who exemplified the splendid and enduring qualities of his forebears – honour, hard work, kindness, caring, gentility, sensitivity and sensibility.

Benjamin Guinness, third Lord Iveagh, was tall and heavily built. Pictures show his benign, round and kindly face. He often wore a faintly perplexed expression, as if he wasn't sure what the question meant. He was shy, extremely polite, self-effacing, courteous, quiet, a gentle man and a gentleman. It was all too easy to think of him as unsure, hesitant, unbusinesslike, but he had an astute mind and he made well-rounded, mature and positive decisions. When pushed to it, he could express his views clearly and decisively.

The job of Chairman was not easy, especially since the third Lord Iveagh did not enjoy good health – he suffered from a particularly virulent form of Crohn's disease – a chronic inflammatory disease of the gastrointestinal tract – and was often in hospital. He was constantly exhausted in his courageous fight to keep it from interfering with his work. An additional problem for the third Lord Iveagh was that he chose not to live in the UK for a five-year period, which made it difficult for him to chair the company. Other family members attended Board meetings in London, but chairing by remote control was not satisfactory.

Like so many of his predecessors, the third Lord Iveagh was involved in a great deal more than just the Company. He was a member of Seanad Éireann, Chairman of the Wright Fleming Institute of Microbiology in London, President of the Multiple Sclerosis Society of Ireland, Hon. Treasurer of the Irish Heart Foundation, Honorary Fellow of the Royal College of Physicians of Ireland. He had farming enterprises in Ireland, England and Canada, was a member of the Irish Turf Club and part-owner of Kildangan Stud in County Kildare. He farmed his 30-acre estate at Farmleigh in County Dublin and he won most of the prizes for cattle at the RDS shows. His personal interests included collecting antique silver, eighteenth-century French drawings and Irish books and bindings.

End of an era

Because of indifferent health, the difficulty of chairing the Company from a distance and extra work brought about by the involvement of the Company with Bells and Distillers, the third Lord Iveagh stepped down as Chairman in 1986, handing over to Ernest Saunders, and accepting a position as President of the Company. It was the first time since the foundation of the Company that the Chairmanship was not in family hands. This was a sad day for Benjamin, for the family and for the Company. The third Lord Iveagh died in 1992, at the age of 55. He is succeeded by his son Arthur Edward Rory as the fourth Lord Iveagh.

All the family seem to have had those qualities I knew so well in the third Lord Iveagh, and their hard-headed business skills were tempered by the way they treated those who worked for them and by their generous acts of philanthropy. As a family, they have stamped their indelible mark and won a place of honour not only in their native Ireland but all over the world. As a family, I am sure they are proud of their achievements, and as a nation, we ought to be proud of them too.

Arthur I
1725–1803

Arthur II
1768–1855

Sir Benjamin Lee, first baronet
1798–1868

Edward Cecil,
first Lord Iveagh
1847–1927

Rupert Edward Cecil,
second Lord Iveagh
1874–1967

Arthur Francis Benjamin,
third Lord Iveagh
1937–1992

Sources

Allen, F H A, *The Iveagh Trust - The First Hundred Years 1890-1990*, Iveagh Trust, 1990

Conaghan, Michael, Oliver Cleeson and Alison Maddock (eds), *The Grand Canal*, OPW , 1982-3

Corran, H S, *A History of Brewing*, David & Charles, 1975

Dennison, S R and Oliver MacDonagh, *Guinness 1896-1939*, Cork University Press, 1998

Guinness, Jonathan, *Requiem for a Family Business*, Macmillan, 1997

The Harp editions from March/April 1958 to spring 1972

Lynch, Patrick and John Vaizey, *Guinness's Brewery in the Irish Economy 1759-1876*, Cambridge University Press, 1960

Mullally, Frederic, *The Silver Salver*, Granada, 1981

St James's Gate Newsletter editions from October 1972 to spring 1978

Seebohm Rowntree, B, *Poverty, A Study of Town Life*, 1901

Sibley, Brian, *The Book of Guinness Advertising*, Guinness Superlatives Ltd, 1985

Welch, Robert, *The Oxford Companion to Irish Literature*, Clarendon Press (Oxford), 1996

Index